AMERICANS' VIEWS
ABOUT WAR

Americans' Views About War

EXAMINING POP CULTURE

JAMES D. TORR
Book Editor

Daniel Leone,
Publisher

Bonnie Szumski,
Editorial Director

Scott Barbour,
Managing Editor

James D. Torr,
Series Editor

Greenhaven Press, Inc.
San Diego, California

Every effort has been made to trace the owners of copyrighted material. The articles in this volume may have been edited for content, length, and/or reading level. The titles have been changed to enhance the editorial purpose.

Library of Congress Cataloging-in-Publication Data

Americans' views about war / James D. Torr, book editor.
    p. cm.—(Examining popular culture)
  Includes bibliographical references and index.
    ISBN 0-7377-0753-4 (pbk. : alk. paper) —
    ISBN 0-7377-0754-2 (lib. bdg. : alk. paper) —
  1. United States—Civilization—20th century. 2. Popular culture—United States—History—20th century. 3. War and society—United States—History—20th century. 4. United States—History, Military—20th century. 5. War—Public opinion. 6. Public opinion—United States.
    I. Torr, James D., 1974–   II. Series.

E169.1 .A526   2002
973.9—dc21   2001023087
                                                                    CIP

Cover Photo: © Bettmann/CORBIS

© 2002 by Greenhaven Press, Inc.
PO Box 28909, San Diego, CA 92198–0990

Printed in the U.S.A.

CONTENTS

effort by producing films that bordered on propaganda.

Chapter 3: The Beginning of the Cold War: The Red Menace and the Nuclear Threat

tee (HUAC) began investigating Hollywood for signs of communist influence, and in response, the major film studios released a series of anticommunist films to restore their image.

Americans have vacillated in their views toward nuclear weapons ever since the atomic bomb was first developed in the 1940s. In general, Americans have been uneasy with their nation's vast nuclear arsenal, and this tension is apparent in popular films from the 1950s to the 1990s.

Chapter 4: The Vietnam War: U.S. Ambivalence Is Reflected in Popular Culture

The war in Vietnam was America's longest, most controversial war and only military defeat, and films about the conflict reflect the multitude of shifting views Americans have held toward it.

In the 1960s popular music became a political weapon in the hands of the peace movement, with antiwar songs such as "I Ain't Marchin' Anymore" and "Eve of Destruction."

The Vietnam War was the first war to be heavily covered by television news reporters. TV audiences were exposed to images of the violence and suffering of the war, and since the war's end historians have debated how television affected popular opinion of the war.

Chapter 5: America Since Vietnam: War Makes a Comeback

FOREWORD

POPULAR CULTURE IS THE COMMON SET OF ARTS, entertainments, customs, beliefs, and values shared by large segments of society. Russel B. Nye, one of the founders of the study of popular culture, wrote that "not until the appearance of mass society in the eighteenth century could popular culture, as one now uses the term, be said to exist." According to Nye, the Industrial Revolution and the rise of democracy in the eighteenth and nineteenth centuries led to increased urbanization and the emergence of a powerful middle class. In nineteenth-century Europe and North America, these trends created audiences for the popular arts that were larger, more concentrated, and more well-off than at any point in history. As a result, more people shared a common culture than ever before.

The technological advancements of the twentieth century vastly accelerated the spread of popular culture. With each new advance in mass communication—motion pictures, radio, television, and the Internet—popular culture has become an increasingly pervasive aspect of everyday life.

Popular entertainment—in the form of movies, television, theater, music recordings and concerts, books, magazines, sporting events, video games, restaurants, casinos, theme parks, and other attractions—is one very recognizable aspect of popular culture. In his 1999 book *The Entertainment Economy: How Mega-Media Forces Are Transforming Our Lives*, Michael J. Wolf argues that entertainment is becoming the dominant feature of American society: "In choosing where we buy French fries, how we relate to political candidates, what airline we want to fly, what pajamas we choose for our kids, and which mall we want to buy them in, entertainment is increasingly influencing every one of those choices. . . . Multiply that by the billions of choices that, collectively, all of us make each day and you have a portrait of a society in which entertainment is one of its leading institutions."

It is partly this pervasive quality of popular culture that makes it worthy of study. James Combs, the author of *Polpop: Politics and Popular Culture in America*, explains that examining popular culture is important because it can shape people's attitudes and beliefs:

> Popular culture is so much a part of our lives that we cannot deny its developmental powers. . . . Like formal education or family rearing, popular culture is part of our "learning environment.". . . Though our pop culture education is informal—we usually do not attend to pop culture for its "educational" value—it nevertheless provides us with information and images upon which we develop our opinions and attitudes. We would not be what we are, nor would our society be quite the same, without the impact of popular culture.

Examining popular culture is also important because popular movies, music, fads, and the like often reflect popular opinions and attitudes. Christopher D. Geist and Jack Nachbar explain in *The Popular Culture Reader*, "the popular arts provide a gauge by which we can learn what Americans are thinking, their fears, fantasies, dreams, and dominant mythologies. The popular arts reflect the values of the multitude."

This two-way relationship between popular culture and society is evident in many modern discussions of popular culture. Does the glorification of guns by many rap artists, for example, merely reflect the realities of inner-city life, or does it also contribute to the problem of gun violence? Such questions also arise in discussions of the popular culture of the past. Did the Vietnam protest music of the late 1960s and early 1970s, for instance, simply reflect popular antiwar sentiments, or did it help turn public opinion against the war? Examining such questions is an important part of understanding history.

Greenhaven Press's Examining Pop Culture series provides students with the resources to begin exploring these questions. Each volume in the series focuses on a particular aspect of popular culture, with topics as varied as popular culture itself. Books in the series may focus on a particular genre, such as *Rap and Hip Hop*, while others may cover a specific medium, such as *Computers and the Internet*. Volumes such as *Body Piercing and Tattoos* have their focus on recent trends in popular culture, while titles like *Americans' Views About War* have a broader historical scope.

In each volume, an introductory essay provides a general

overview of the topic. The selections that follow offer a survey of critical thought about the subject. The readings in *Americans' Views About War*, for example, are arranged chronologically: Essays explore how popular films, songs, television programs, and even comic books both reflected and shaped public opinion about American wars from World War I through Vietnam. The essays in *Violence in Film and TV*, on the other hand, take a more varied approach: Some provide historical background, while others examine specific genres of violent film, such as horror, and still others discuss the current controversy surrounding the issue.

Each book in the series contains a comprehensive index to help readers quickly locate material of interest. Perhaps most importantly, each volume has an annotated bibliography to aid interested students in conducting further research on the topic. In today's culture, what is "popular" changes rapidly from year to year and even month to month. Those who study popular culture must constantly struggle to keep up. The volumes in Greenhaven's Examining Pop Culture series are intended to introduce readers to the major themes and issues associated with each topic, so they can begin examining for themselves what impact popular culture has on their own lives.

INTRODUCTION

FASCINATION WITH WAR IS CERTAINLY NOT unique to America or Americans. "Stories of men in combat have captivated audiences since the days of Homer," notes film critic Lenny Rubenstein. War has often been associated with adventure and heroism; combat has been viewed as a way for men to prove their masculinity and experience the thrill of challenging death. But like audiences in other times and places, Americans have been torn between this romantic view of war and the knowledge that, as the saying goes, "war is hell." War entails death and destruction. Combat is less glorious and more brutal than is often imagined, and wars often fail to bring about lasting peace or change.

Ambivalence Toward War in Popular Culture

This ambivalence toward war is a major theme in popular culture, particularly in popular films. "The paradox of glorifying war while opposing war itself finds no better expression than in Hollywood itself," writes Lawrence H. Suid in *Guts & Glory: Great American War Films*. "Virtually all filmmakers claim to be against war and militarism. They maintain that their war movies portray antiwar messages, usually through the 'war is hell' theme." But, Suid notes, war films often serve less as a warning against the horrors of war than as a way for audiences to vicariously experience the thrill of battle: "Planes, bombs, guns, the destruction they cause, the very elements that filmmakers believe show the evil of war ultimately provide the attraction that makes war films so popular."

The appeal of war stories is similar to other forms of popular entertainment. "For a very long time," notes James Combs, an author and former professor of political science, "the only way non-combatants could experience war was through story-telling that was decidedly second-hand and after the fact. People would listen to 'war stories' told by returning veterans or read books that gave fictional or factual accounts of the war." Veterans still tell war stories, and many novels, both great and forgettable, examine the soldier's experience of war. In the visual media, artists have painted large murals of famous battles, attempting to convey the feeling of "being there," and modern photojournalists have tried to capture the essence of combat.

Movies, whether they be wartime documentaries or Hollywood dramas, have merely allowed for a more visceral representation of battle. "The motion picture gave kinetic power to our imagination of warfare as no medium . . . had ever done before," writes Combs. The enduring popularity of war films, according to Suid, "attests to the degree to which Hollywood has successfully captured the atmosphere of combat."

Shifting Views of War in American History

While Americans generally hold ambivalent views toward war, being both drawn to and repelled by stories of battle and bloodshed, public opinion on specific wars has depended largely on the circumstances of each conflict. Thus Americans' willingness to go to war has waxed and waned throughout the nation's history, a shift correspondingly reflected in popular culture. Because the major mass media—print newspapers and magazines, radio, movies, and television—are largely twentieth-century phenomena, reflections of Americans' views about war in popular entertainment are more evident for recent conflicts. Many social critics also point out that, as the mass media have become more and more integral to Americans' daily lives, popular culture increasingly has the ability to *influence* Americans' opinions about war as well as reflect them.

The first major conflict of the twentieth century was World War I. Due to the intense nationalism, economic rivalry, and military alliances present in Europe at the time, the hostilities following the assassination of the heir to the Austrian and Hungarian thrones in July 1914 quickly escalated into a full-scale war, with Great Britain, France, Russia, Italy, and other Allied powers opposing the Central powers of Germany, Austria-Hungary, Turkey, and Bulgaria. The United States initially tried to maintain a position of neutrality, but the sinking of the unarmed British liner *Lusitania* and the French steamer *Sussex* by German submarines led to U.S. protests against Germany's use of submarine warfare to deter commerce between the United States and Great Britain. On April 6, 1917, a divided

U.S. Congress accepted President Woodrow Wilson's declaration of war against the Central powers.

Once the United States officially joined the Allies, Americans embraced the war effort with patriotic zeal. The shift in public opinion, from isolationism to "war fever," is perhaps most evident in the popular songs of the era. In 1915 and 1916, one of the most popular songs in America was the vaudeville musical number "I Didn't Raise My Boy to Be a Soldier"; after U.S. entry into the war, parodies such as "I Didn't Raise My Boy to Be a Coward" quickly emerged. The day after the declaration of war was signed, Broadway producer-songwriter George M. Cohan composed his pro-war anthem "Over There," which soon became "one of the most popular war songs of all times," according to historian M. Paul Holsinger.

However, another shift in public opinion was evident a few years after the war's end in 1918, this time from patriotic optimism to postwar disillusionment. Over four years of conflict and 37 million casualties had done much to dull the initial enthusiasm for the fight. The United States suffered relatively few casualties (approximately 350,000) because of its late entry into the war, but nevertheless shared in the antiwar sentiment that emerged in the 1920s. "Veterans returned with scars and stories of battle," writes Combs, "and the promise of peace turned out to be a dismal failure." As a result, he notes, war films of the 1920s and early 1930s "took the view that the Great War had been a grave mistake, and that the sacrifices on all sides had not been worth it."

Popular Culture During World War II

American antiwar sentiment lasted little more than a decade. The tide of public opinion began to change again with Japan's attack on China in July 1937 and Nazi Germany's invasion of Poland in September 1939. Though the United States again officially claimed a position of neutrality, President Franklin Roosevelt warned repeatedly of the threat posed by the totalitarian governments of Germany, Italy, and Japan, collectively known as the Axis powers. Americans were supportive of their unofficial allies in the European war, and when Japan attacked the American Pacific Fleet in Hawaii on December 7, 1941, the United States officially entered World War II. As in World

War I, popular entertainment also "went to war" with marked eagerness.

In the popular entertainment of the 1940s, World War II was everywhere—thousands of books, stories, songs, and artworks about the conflict were created during the war years alone. Sports commentators adopted war imagery in their descriptions of boxing matches and football games. Hollywood studios, working partly in cooperation with the federal government, released war films that emphasized the rightness of the Allied cause, the importance of victory, and the courage of men in uniform. In his book *In the Shadow of War*, historian Michael Shelly notes how even advertising adopted wartime themes: "'Anyone buying a new Plymouth today,' ran one ad, 'has the satisfaction of not only obtaining the finest car in Plymouth history, but of knowing he has also given support to the defense production structure.'"

This abundance of war-themed entertainment was due in part to the fact that the mass media were more prominent than they had been in World War I. By the 1940s, radios had become common in American homes, and the movie industry had grown enormously and achieved several technical innovations, including the addition of sound in the late 1920s. Because American factory production was crucial to the Allied cause, civilians too were much more a part of the war effort than they had been in World War I. In an April 1942 address Roosevelt emphasized the need for all Americans to be committed to the war effort: "One front and one battle where everyone in the United States—every man, woman and child—is in action. That front is right here at home, in our daily lives." The pervasiveness of war themes in popular culture played a key role in rallying the homefront. As Sherry explains, "More than at any other time in their history, a consciousness of shared experience gave Americans an intangible but powerful unity."

The Cold War

Unlike the post–World War I period, no outspoken pacifist movement followed the end of World War II. In part this was because the United States suddenly found itself with new enemies: the Soviet Union and its ally, the People's Republic of

China. Though they had been Allies in World War II, these nations' communist ideology was fundamentally at odds with the capitalist democracies of the United States, Great Britain, and other Western European countries.

The Cold War that dominated international relations for the next four decades was essentially a state of enmity, tension, and war-readiness between the United States and the Soviet Union. Although the Cold War was not a war in the traditional sense, Americans readily substituted anticommunist for anti-Nazi sentiment. The beginning of the Cold War was marked by suspicion—and in some cases paranoia—that communists were infiltrating the U.S. government in an attempt to subvert national security. Fears about communist subversion—of otherwise normal-looking Americans in league with an enemy force—were explored allegorically in films such as *Invasion of the Body Snatchers* (1956), in which pods from outer space replace the inhabitants of a small town with imposters.

The government took an active role in opposing communist subversion with the House Un-American Activities Committee (HUAC), which investigated suspected communist sympathizers. After HUAC targeted the film industry in the late 1940s, Hollywood released several blatantly anticommunist films in an effort to restore its patriotic image. Portrayals of communism in popular culture, according to historian Daniel J. Leab, tended to "emphasize the supposedly overwhelming attractiveness of American values and way of life, and condemn the evil, atheistic heartlessness of communism and the drab quality of life in countries under its brutal sway." Antiwar themes were confined to less serious genres such as science fiction. In 1951's *The Day the Earth Stood Still*, for example, a benevolent alien with a giant robot attempts to force the United Nations to adopt world peace.

In 1950 Americans entered the Cold War's first "hot war." From 1950 to 1953 the United States was one of twenty nations engaged in a limited international war in Korea. Ostensibly between North and South Korea, the conflict was actually a by-product of the Cold War, with the Soviet Union and China backing North Korea and the United States and the United Nations supporting South Korea. Although over 2 million Americans were sent to the front lines in Korea, it was always a limited war. To avoid a full-scale war between the superpowers, neither the United States nor the Soviet Union committed its full military strength. The United States and its allies dominated the fight and this bolstered Americans' confidence that the West would ultimately prevail over communism.

This confidence, though, was tempered by a growing fear of what an unlimited war between the newly emergent superpowers would entail. The invention of nuclear weapons during World War II had initially been received with some optimism in the United States. The bomb had been used to force Japan's surrender in 1945, and for years afterward atomic-themed toys, comic books, and even restaurants enjoyed fad status. But Americans' excitement was dampened when the Soviets exploded an atomic weapon of their own in 1949, and soon fascination with the splitting of the atom gave way to dark predictions that the next world war could end in nuclear Armageddon. Films such as *Dr. Strangelove* and *Fail-Safe*, both released in 1964, depicted the Cold War arms race ending in nuclear disaster.

Vietnam

While *Dr. Strangelove* sent a potent message about the dangers of the arms race, the film was very much a black comedy: It blatantly ridiculed Cold War "hawks" (who support the use of military force, as opposed to "doves" who press for peace). That such a film could even be made in 1964 shows just how ambivalent the nation's mood toward the Cold War had become. One reason Americans were once again growing wary of war was the escalating conflict in Vietnam.

The Vietnam War, like the Korean War, was a limited international conflict in which the United States and the Soviet Union attempted to steer a Third World nation toward or away from communism. U.S. involvement in Vietnam had begun in 1950, when President Harry Truman sent advisers to aid French colonial South Vietnam in its war against the newly formed government of North Vietnam. After China and the Soviet Union began to openly support North Vietnam, Presidents Dwight Eisenhower and John F. Kennedy escalated U.S. aid to South Vietnam.

In 1965 President Lyndon Johnson sent the first U.S.

ground forces to South Vietnam; that year also marked the beginning of the turn in public opinion against the war. The reasons for the growing U.S. opposition to the Vietnam War are complex, but one explanation centers around the use of guerrilla warfare by procommunist South Vietnamese fighters known as the Vietcong, who cooperated with the North Vietnamese. Avoiding pitched battles, guerrilla fighters used hit-and-run attacks and hid among the civilian population, making it hard for U.S. troops to know who or where the enemy was. By 1967 almost four hundred thousand U.S. troops were in Vietnam, but America's sophisticated army could not eradicate the guerrilla forces.

Another key factor behind the U.S. antiwar movement of the late 1960s was the television coverage of the war. Press reporting during the world wars had been limited to news and radio; movie newsreels during World War II were produced by the government and heavily edited to give a positive view of the war's progress; even in Korea, journalists inside the war zone were subject to heavy censorship. By the 1960s, however, more Americans depended on television for their news. The military was less able to control the hundreds of members of the international press corps. As a result, Vietnam became America's "living room war": Each night audiences were exposed to images of combat and casualties that were far more graphic than in previous wars.

The demoralizing effects of guerrilla warfare culminated in the Tet offensive of 1968, in which the North Vietnamese and Vietcong attacked thirty-six major cities and towns in South Vietnam. Although the North Vietnamese suffered very heavy casualties during the offensive, Americans watching the war from home were shocked by the brutality of the fighting and became convinced that the war in Vietnam was unwinnable. Pressure mounted on President Johnson, and his successor, Richard Nixon, to end the war. Here, too, the media played a major role: "How many marches and demonstrations would we have if the marchers did not know that the ever-faithful TV cameras would be there to record their antics?" complained Vice President Spiro Agnew in 1969.

In March 1968 Johnson promised an end to the bombing of North Vietnam, and from 1969 to 1973 President Nixon oversaw a slow and halting, but ultimately complete, with-drawal of U.S. troops from Vietnam. Although Nixon claimed that "peace with honor" had been achieved in Vietnam, most Americans felt that the United States had lost its first war, a feeling that was confirmed when the government of South Vietnam finally fell in July 1976 and Vietnam was united as the Socialist Republic of Vietnam.

The Vietnam War was a severe blow to American national pride, and the Vietnam experience has been a powerful subject in popular entertainment ever since. In books, film, and tele-vision, the Vietnam War and Vietnam vets have been glorified, vilified, and used as metaphors. Most of the popular entertain-ment of the 1970s, '80s, and '90s that deals with war at all deals with the Vietnam War. Some social critics feel that the deba-cle in Vietnam still colors most Americans' views of war, leav-ing the nation on the whole reluctant to commit to interna-tional conflicts.

However, as history shows, Americans tend not to stay pacifists for very long. Similarly, the history of American pop-ular culture indicates that Americans' inclination toward ei-ther war or peace is often reflected in the most popular enter-tainments of the day. The essays in Examining Pop Culture: *Americans' Views About War* are intended to provide a histori-cal survey of how American popular culture has reflected, and in some cases shaped, Americans' views about war. By explor-ing how Americans have alternately embraced and rejected war throughout the twentieth century, it is hoped that the reader might better understand the ambiguous views that Americans still hold toward war today.

PROLOGUE

Americans Discover the Horrors of Modern Warfare

A Brief History of America's View of War

Michael S. Sherry

War has played a fundamental role in American history, and Americans themselves have long held mixed views toward it. During the Revolutionary War, for example, Americans celebrated the independence they won but at the same time distrusted the power of the military and deplored the carnage of battle. In the nineteenth century, advances in technology encouraged a more optimistic view of war, as inventors and military strategists promised new weapons and tactics that would enable the nation to enjoy the fruits of war with minimal bloodshed. The Civil War had a profound effect on the nation's view of armed conflict. The devastating effects of the Civil War, coupled with America's geographical isolation from Europe, left Americans much more worried about domestic strife than they were about enemies abroad. World War I would change that view.

Michael S. Sherry is a professor of history at Northwestern University who focuses on the relationship between military force and American foreign policy. The following essay is excerpted from his 1995 book *In the Shadow of War: The United States Since the 1930s*.

WAR CREATED THE UNITED STATES. ALTHOUGH many Americans professed genuine hostility toward it, war was

■

central to their history, the instrument by which they forged and expanded their nation and often defined themselves.

The Creation and Expansion of the United States

The American Revolution was itself a war, often a nasty one. It broke out in part over military issues—the fiscal burdens, intrusive presence, and ideological threat many Americans perceived in English military ambitions and institutions. It presented the rebels with a dilemma that would persist in American history: How could they wage war against the evils of militarism without creating them in their own midst? And it left Americans in a tenuous military condition; despite their victory, reliable defense of the nation's borders was in doubt for three decades.

Politics and folklore sustained the centrality of war for Americans long after the Revolution. No figures loomed larger in political mythology than George Washington, the warrior President, and Abraham Lincoln, the war President. From Washington through Teddy Roosevelt, former military officers seized the presidential nominations of their parties and often the presidency itself. The Revolution and the Civil War remained touchstones of national memory, their meanings repeatedly plumbed and refashioned. A nation born in war, threatened by invasion, expanded through conquest, and finally reconceived in civil war, owed much to Mars.

True, it paid its debt grudgingly. Americans often celebrated what war gained them, but rarely war's institutions and burdens. Their distrust of professional "standing armies"—of their origins in a decadent Europe, of their power to corrupt or overawe the Republic—was deep. The new nation sanctioned only a bare-bones, decentralized military force. It relied on the voluntary enthusiasm of amateurs—men Washington described as "just dragged from the tender scenes of domestick life" and all too "ready to fly from their own shadows"—and hence also on the coercion of ideological fervor rather than the compulsion of the state to wage its wars. And although military service added attractive plumage to a political candidate, military officers as a class did not gain great social prestige or telling political clout. From the outset, then, a deep ambivalence pervaded American attitudes toward war and its institutions: dependence on both matched distrust of each.

The armed forces nonetheless played a telling role in defending, expanding, and building the new nation. As if to resolve their ambivalence, Americans liked their military forces best when they undertook decidedly unmilitary functions. President Thomas Jefferson established the United States Military Academy at West Point less as a schoolhouse in destruction than as an academy of science and engineering, the role it played for decades in a nation hell-bent on internal development but lacking institutions with the requisite expertise. Army officers like Meriwether Lewis and William Clark surveyed the West and searched out its scientific secrets. Academy graduates, either in uniform or after entering private business, helped to build bridges, canals, harbors, and railroads. They were happy to do so, seeing in that role, rather than in war making, their main hope for gaining social prestige and economic security. Their efforts forged a lasting link between the armed forces and the nation's economic and technological development. That link went further. The army's Harpers Ferry and Springfield arsenals pioneered standardized mass production. In the 1840s, Congress debated how development of iron-clad warships might nourish the iron industry. Later, businessmen and technical experts gleaned the Civil War's record for lessons on how to rationalize the burgeoning corporate economy.

The American Vision of War

During the nineteenth century, Americans also developed their particular, though not unique, style of imagining and waging war. American officers favored a "strategy of annihilation" entailing head-on assaults against an enemy's armed forces or productive capacity, rather than limited campaigns of movement, surprise, or attrition. It was a brutal style of war waged against Native Americans and in the Civil War, when many Americans embraced war's destructiveness as an instrument of higher causes and took "flight into unreason: into visions of purgation and redemption, into anticipation and intuition and spiritual apotheosis, into bloodshed that was not only intentional pursuit of interests of state but was also sacramental, erotic, mystical, and strangely gratifying [according to Charles Royster in his book *The Destructive War*]." Wars of annihilation drew on such attitudes, and on the capacity to mass produce weapons and war materiel and the locomotives and ships to move them. The system was synergistic, if rarely seen as such: the armed forces spurred economic development, which in turn enhanced American military power.

Some Americans carried this vision further. Developing the "cult of the superweapon," they imagined stunning new weapons enabling the nation to usher in a Pax Americana by smashing its enemies or by making war too hellish to be waged, so that "war shall cease to desolate the world nor burning cities mark its dreadful track," as the inventor Robert Fulton hoped. By century's end, the notion was commonplace that submarines, airships, or other devices might deter or humanize war, despite doubts about what would happen if the magical weapon belonged instead to an enemy, or got used in a civil war among Americans, or made killing too easy rather than too horrific. Mark Twain savagely mocked the vision of American weapons making peace in *A Connecticut Yankee in King Arthur's Court* (1889), a comic nightmare of automated butchery in battle. But dreams of triumphal American technology continued to hold sway. They tapped Americans' ambivalence about war, promising that the nation could gain what it wanted from war through superior technology rather than through the dreadful leviathan of large standing armies.

The Civil War's Legacy

Imagining future wars, Americans also continued to plumb the meaning of past ones—above all the Civil War, which gripped the American imagination so long in part because a half-century went by before another major war. Americans judged politicians by their wartime heroism and waved the "bloody shirt" in political campaigns. They employed war as a metaphor for other struggles, as in one scholar's *History of the Warfare of Science and Theology in Christendom*. They compared the Civil War's attractive model of idealism, discipline, and self-sacrifice to the rank materialism, squalid corruption, and corporate giantism of post–Civil War America. Few Civil War veterans wanted another war or joined Oliver Wendell Holmes, Jr., in urging Americans "to pray, not for comfort, but for combat." But many Americans joined Teddy Roosevelt in celebrating the strenuous and democratizing virtues of wartime service. Or they tried to extract the virtues of war from war itself. Champions of civil service reform drew on an "ideal of military professionalism." Social reformers saw charity work as akin to enlisting in an army at war, now "with vice and poverty as the enemy." Edward Bellamy's *Looking Backward* (1888) imagined a utopia at peace but operated by a disciplined army of workers. In 1910 came the crowning appeal to exploit war's virtues in peacetime, William James's "The Moral Equivalent of War." James proposed to rekindle the Civil War spirit by drafting youth into an "army against nature" whose soldiers would dig coal, wash dishes, erect skyscrapers, and generally "get the childishness knocked out of them"—a proposal often seen as a precursor to the New Deal's Civilian Conservation Corps and John Kennedy's Peace Corps. Views like James's, although easily seen as opposed to the bellicose militarism of a Teddy Roosevelt, in fact only bent similar assumptions to different purposes. James, too, believed that "militarism is the great preserver of our ideals of hardihood."

Reflections on the Civil War also emerged amid fears of a new war (for which the Paris Commune of 1871 served as a frightening model) that might pit the nation's social classes, racial or ethnic groups, or ideological factions against each other. Indeed, military forces repeatedly intervened on the side of the new corporate giants to subdue striking workers, just as embattled workers saw themselves as "industrial armies" and marched in 1894 as "Coxey's Army." Afraid of the enraged masses, prominent Americans proposed an expanded army to garrison cities—arguments more successfully used for modernizing state militias, or the National Guard, as collectively they came to be called. From a different vantage point, authors of apocalyptic visions—Twain in *Connecticut Yankee*, Ignatius Donnelly in *Caesar's Column* (1890)—cast war as a civil conflict harnessing dreadful new weapons to internal passions. Although fear of class war abated after the century's turn, champions of preparedness claimed that universal military service would close the fissures of class and ethnicity by giving all boys a common discipline and training in democracy's virtues.

For Americans fearing domestic strife, the Civil War had resonance. It loomed over succeeding generations just as World

War II did over later generations fearing another international war. The great class war never erupted, just as World War III never broke out, but in both cases skirmishes in the imagined war—conflicts with labor in the late 1800s, the "limited wars" of Korea and Vietnam—kept the specter alive. In such ways, war occupied a central place in America's earlier history, as in our own times.

War Was a Distant Threat

But the similarities cannot be pushed very far. Above all, after the War of 1812 the new nation enjoyed remarkable immunity from attack, though not the "free security" that nostalgic Americans in the mid-twentieth century imagined. Border disputes, threats to trade, Native Americans' resistance to conquest, and growing imperial ambitions offered real challenges. But it was with reason that young Abraham Lincoln could ask in 1837, "Shall we expect some transatlantic military giant to step the ocean and crush us at a blow?" and answer boastfully, "Never! All the armies of Europe, Asia, and Africa combined . . . could not by force take a drink from the Ohio or make a track on the Blue Ridge in a trial of a thousand years." The only serious threat to the nation, Lincoln recognized, came from within it.

A term like "national security," implying broad and continuous efforts to defend a country, as yet had no place. The United States maintained a *War* Department (and a Navy Department)—not yet a Defense Department and a National Security Council—a designation suggesting that war was an episodic event, not the object of sustained anxiety. War intruded only occasionally into the lives of Americans, and when it did occur, its circumstances (except for the Civil War) allowed leaders great latitude about whether to participate. The Civil War loomed over the American imagination, but as a site of contested memories about a bitter division, not as the touchstone of national unity against a foreign threat. It therefore lacked the resonance with world events that World War II would hold for Americans. Few nineteenth-century Americans saw their nation's fortunes as bound up with distant wars in a seamless world and as dependent on massive military power. What became war's constant shadow was then only a passing eclipse. . . .

Until well into the twentieth century national defense claimed only a minor part of the nation's resources. War imposed enormous burdens, but defense as an ongoing activity did not. Despite blood-curdling expressions of militaristic sentiment from some Americans, militarization as a grand historical process was at most incipient, well behind the stage it had reached in Europe.

The forces were nonetheless gathering to advance that process in America. War's democratization, industrialization, and professionalization were often seen in the nineteenth century as likely to make war more humane and less frequent, but those developments, tied as they were to that century's powerful nationalism and imperialism, only prepared the way for the titanic warfare of the twentieth century. Europe was caught up in an arms race bearing down on and sucking in the rest of the world.

Expansion of the Armed Forces

Americans responded to that arms race with a confused and limited expansion of their own armed forces. Some chastised Old World militarism, but others were eager to join the race, especially its showy competition in battleship navies. No single ideological viewpoint or cluster of interest drove the growth of American arms. Because many anti-imperialists were also virulently anti-British, for example, they supported a big American navy able to challenge the world's largest fleet or expand American commerce. While industrialists pressed for contracts and scientists like Thomas Edison promised amazing weapons, their efforts to secure defense monies had only limited results in the absence of intense interservice rivalries or widespread alarms about the nation's safety. What drove military modernization and expansion at its critical stage during the Roosevelt and Taft presidencies was a small coalition of patrician civilians like Elihu Root, Henry L. Stimson, and Roosevelt himself, and reformers within the officer corps.

Still, their calculations of interest did not alone propel modernization and expansion. Only occasionally, and then not very plausibly, did reformers cite territorial safety as justification. They also wanted military power in order to support American hegemony over a world-capitalist economy, but that argument too was strained and episodic. Military institutions were [, according to military historian Walter Millis,] "organic growths developing, as do most great social institutions, out of complex soils of vested interests, political and economic ambitions, unanalyzed fears and untested assumptions about historical causation." Like Roosevelt, many Americans believed that military power expressed more than it underwrote the nation's ascendancy: big nations needed big navies and the expansion that went with them, "or we are not great" and face only "stagnation and decay," so naval officers could argue. That view prevailed easily before World War I, when war, at least in its horrific forms, seemed remote, so that the nation's new engines of war [in the words of historian Thomas C. Leonard] "were thought of simply as beautiful pieces of machinery completely unconnected with the destruction of human life"—symbols of national pride and technological achievement. The growth of American arms also proceeded because the resources to realize it were abundant, and because Progressive reformers admired effective national government and saw armed forces as an expression of it.

The ease with which the armed forces expanded allowed for substantial confusion about ultimate purposes. A convenient war, as with Spain in 1898, or a convenient war scare, as with Japan during Teddy Roosevelt's presidency, provided pretext but little compelling reason for the armed forces' growth. Economic and territorial imperialism, strategic anxieties, nationalism and racism, elitist longings to enhance the nation's internal cohesion, attraction to darkly determinist notions—such impulses behind expansion thrived in a climate where none was severely tested and at force levels still so low that few Americans needed to worry about joining Europe's powers in the abyss of war and militarism.

Americans did peer into that abyss during World War I, which marked a watershed in their relationship to war. Mindful of Europe's methods of total war, American political, business, and military leaders constructed a national machinery for harnessing resources. Manpower, industry, science, food, trade, and opinion were conscripted into service, as war's democratization yielded its paradoxical results: war in the name of the people sanctioned their mobilization and death at unimaginable levels.

Pacifism in Popular Culture: Antiwar Films After World War I

Thomas Doherty

When World War I began Hollywood initially embraced it. Many films produced during the war, especially in 1917 and 1918 when the United States officially entered the conflict, reflected official propaganda. The films portrayed Americans and the Allies as heroic, while Germans were depicted as "Huns"—monstrous enemies of civilization.

This wartime enthusiasm, however, soon gave way to disillusionment, and by the 1920s many Americans viewed the Great War as a mistake. This antiwar sentiment was captured in pacifist-themed film and literature. Perhaps the most famous of the latter is Erich Maria Remarque's 1929 novel *All Quiet on the Western Front*, which depicts the horrors of trench warfare and questions the nationalism that led to the conflict. A film adaptation of Remarque's novel followed in 1930, and it was just one of many antiwar films released in the 1920s and 1930s. The view that war is hell dominated popular film until the eve of World War II.

Thomas Doherty is a professor of American Studies at Brandeis University. The following selection is excerpted from his book *Projections of War: Hollywood, American Culture, and World War II*. He is also the

■

Excerpted from Thomas Doherty, *Projections of War: Hollywood, American Culture, and World War II* (New York: Columbia University Press, 1993). Copyright © 1993 by Columbia University Press. Reprinted by permission of the publisher via the Copyright Clearance Center.

author of *Teenagers and Teenpics: The Juvenilization of American Movies in the 1950s* and the associate editor of the film journal *Cineaste*.

IN 1917, DISGUSTED BY THE WAR FEVER GRIPPING America, the critic Randolph Bourne reminded his countrymen that "the real enemy is War not imperial Germany." The heady hurrahs and ardent patriotism of the early months of the American entry into the European maelstrom not only crushed progressive hopes for pan-national socialism but worse still had found artists and intellectuals willingly succumbing to the war mania. "There is work to be done," Bourne warned, "to prevent this war of ours from passing into popular mythology as a holy crusade." Bourne himself—dead in 1918 of another fever, the influenza pandemic—never lived to hear his solitary voice of dissent become the common chorus. Yet no sooner was the Armistice signed than Bourne's work was taken up by historians, writers, and filmmakers. From 1918 until the eve of the Second World War, the popular mythology of the Great War—memoirs, novels, stage plays, and movies—derided the Wilsonian idealism and debunked the holy crusade.

The motion picture industry followed the course of Bourne's weak-willed artists: during the war, a willing participant; after the war, a penitent erasing its own complicity. Where the war years from 1914 to 1918 had witnessed the embryonic medium's formal entry into the art of war, the retrospective films of the interwar years from 1919 to 1939 projected the futility of combat and the nobility of pacifism. The Great War was seldom a preferred subject for film treatment much less the direct celebration later engendered by the Second World War. The carnage was so brutal and senseless, the outcome so shattering and disorienting, that it resisted celluloid rehabilitation. Hollywood never engineered the raw materials of the Great War—destruction, death, and disillusionment—into the scaffolding for durable generic construction—reconciliation, reassurance, affirmation. On screen, the main lesson of the "War to End All Wars" was to end all wars. . . .

The Great War created a ravenous market for moving pictures of mobilization and combat. Early newsreels ("the week-lies") and screen magazines reported back from the front with the promise of *War As It Really Is* (1916) and *The Horrors of War* (1916). Not infrequently, the attacking soldiers were a throng of extras dodging explosions set off by technicians, a brazen violation of the boundary between news and drama that was almost unknown in the next war. . . .

Limiting itself to a consideration of "outstanding films," a trade survey of motion picture content traced the rising tide of war-on-screen. "The early years of the war, prior to America's entry, found the screen offering less than 10 per cent of war coloration, with but two war subjects in the 1914–1915 period, none during 1915–1916, and eight in 1916–1917." In 1917–18, however, Hollywood produced twenty-three major war films, or 26 percent of a total of eighty-nine productions. Moreover, "in 1918, from September through December, the proportion rose. There were 15 war pictures among the 35 listed or 43 per cent of the total for that period." For the first time also fiction films incorporated frontline footage into narratives for purposes of authenticity and impact, notably in D.W. Griffith's *Hearts of the World* (1918). Anti-German melodramas featuring a marauding Rupert Julian or a monocled Erich von Stroheim ("the man you love to hate," salivated taglines) dominate the archival record. Even by the standards of 1917–18, *Escaping the Hun*, *To Hell with the Kaiser!* and *The Kaiser, the Beast of Berlin*, where frothing Huns violate Belgian virgins and defenestrate squalling infants, were crudely fantastical. They served to discredit not only the portrayal of war on screen but the whole enterprise of cinematic propaganda.

After the Armistice, during the interwar period that witnessed the consolidation of studio-system dominance and the full flowering of motion picture art, Hollywood atoned for its excesses. The memory of the Great War, preserved, distorted, and measured by Hollywood film before 1941, contrasts strikingly with subsequent recollections. Picturesque violence aside, the retrospective Great War film produced *prior* to World War II was elegiac in tone, pacifist in purpose, and cynical in perspective. Like the poetry of Ezra Pound, the memoirs of e.e. cummings, and the fiction of Ernest Hemingway, the films make a separate peace.

The Big Parade

The first of the antiwar epics, MGM's *The Big Parade*, held its gala premiere at Grauman's Egyptian Theatre on November 11, 1925, a widely covered event that foretold a perennial difficulty in deeming war simultaneously intolerable as experience and irresistible as spectacle. In the days when full stage shows served as prologue to major motion pictures, Grauman's devised a pageant entitled "Memories of 1918" to precede the premiere screening. Featuring a medley of martial tunes, a series of posed "historical tableaux," and an elaborate "danse militaire" (twenty-four chorus girls doing "a high-stepping, kicking, dancing military routine"), the original preshow extravaganza climaxed on a telling miscalculation. A reporter from *Variety* described the last moments of the live warm-up:

> For the finale, "The Unknown Soldier" was the tableau on the opening performance. It had a catafalque with two soldiers guarding the flag-draped bier in the shadows of the Capital at Washington. It was beautiful and impressive but for a climax held the audience in reverence on account of [the] forceful impressiveness of the symbol it conveyed, with the result it did not leave such a pleasant taste in the mouth of the patrons for the beginning of the picture, as well as denying them their commendation to Grauman for his wonderful achievement. [That is, to applaud would have been disrespectful.]

That bad taste in the collective mouth was the bitter fruit of the late war, a funereal memory evoked all too vividly by the military pageant within a pageant. For successive performances, the showstopper was made more palatable. After the initial misstep, the flag-draped catafalque was taken out, "with the Presentation of the Colors of the Allies" being used to close the show and "get the big applause the presentation deserved."

Thus primed, audiences for *The Big Parade* saw the cinematic equivalent of the disillusioning literature, a wasteland of meaningless death yoked uncertainly to conventional romance. Director King Vidor's stated intent was to deglamorize warfare. Like Stephen Crane in *The Red Badge of Courage*, he sought to depict war from the mud of the trenches instead of the chambers of the General Staff. Matinee idol John Gilbert

World War I Propaganda Films

Although the use of propaganda films can be traced back as far as the Spanish-American War, it was not until the outbreak of the First World War in Europe that American political figures realized the value of the motion picture as a propaganda tool. . . .

The first such feature, and the most important, was *The Battle Cry of Peace*, based on Hudson Maxim's book, *Defenseless America*. . . . The film, which unfortunately has not survived, was devastating in its depiction of an America unprepared for war and overrun by a Germanic-looking army, which pillages and rapes, and at the close leaves the Capitol in ruins.

At its premiere in New York on September 9, 1916, a celebrity-packed audience heard attacks on the song, "I Didn't Raise My Boy to Be a Soldier," and a letter from Roosevelt in which he urged that "the duty of military service should be as widespread as the right to vote." The Daughters of the American Revolution arranged for a special presentation of the film for Congress, but President Wilson declined to attend.

As a result in part not only of the continuing preparedness movement in the United States, but also because *The Battle Cry of Peace* was a commercial success, further films along similar lines were planned. . . .

With America's entry into the First World War, the use of films for propaganda purposes was officially recognized by the U.S. Government. On September 15, 1917, the United States Government Committee on Public Information: Division of Films was established. It produced a weekly newsreel, *The Official War Review*, as well as three feature-length propaganda documentaries, *Pershing's Crusaders* (1918), *America's Answer* (1918) and *Under Four Flags* (1919).

Anthony Slide, "American Propaganda Films of the First World War," in David Platt, ed., *Celluloid Power*, 1992.

plays James Apperson, the wealthy scion of a mill owner, who enlists in a flurry of nationalistic fervor and oedipal rebellion. In the Army he mixes with the lower orders, Bull (Tom O'Brien), a beefy Irish bartender, and Slim (Karl Dane), a lanky, tobacco-chewing ironworker. All learn that no one wins in the patriot's game. Karl and Bull die bloody deaths and James returns home missing a leg. James learns too that the enemy soldiers on the other side of the concertina wire are his kinsmen. Sharing a cigarette with a dying German, James sees an enemy transformed into a man no different from himself.

The bestial Hun was suddenly a fraternal friend—sometimes literally so. In John Ford's *Four Sons* (1928) an American soldier hears the chilling cries of a German moaning "mutterchen" across no-man's-land. "I guess they gots mothers too," admits a doughboy in intertitle. Unable to stand the lament, a Yank goes over the top to offer the Hun comfort. A beautiful tracking shot follows the Samaritan's course through the mist and wire, to the source of the sound, his enemy, his real-life brother.

All Quiet on the Western Front

The next landmark antiwar film arose from Erich Maria Remarque's international bestseller, *All Quiet on the Western Front*. Originally published in German in 1928, the worldwide success of *Im Westen Nichts Neues* [the book's German title] was extraordinary not only because it gave the enemy a human face but because Americans were so disposed to recognize it as their own. In Universal-International's $1,200,000 adaptation, directed by Lewis Milestone and released in 1930, the avuncular scrounger Katczinsky (Louis Wolheim) suggests a diplomatic solution to war. "You should take all the kings and their cabinets and their generals, put 'em in the center [of a big field] dressed in their underpants and let 'em fight it out with clubs." His fellow troops, and Depression audiences, grumbled their assent.

All Quiet on the Western Front begins in sound and fury. Massing troops and blaring martial music drown out a high school professor's lecture. What looks at first like ironic commentary, the frenzy of war smothering the voice of learning, is in fact complicity not juxtaposition. The teacher exhorts his young charges to be "gay heroes" for the fatherland, to enlist as one in the name of patriotism and school spirit. In a dizzying Eisensteinian montage of close-ups, the boys jump to the bait.

Exploiting the comparative freedom of expression in the pre-Code era [before the Office of War Information began monitoring film content during World War II], *All Quiet on the Western Front* shoots down the transcendence of storybook battle with the flatulence of ground-level reality. The raw recruits are beset by hunger, rats, lice, and loss of sphincter control. Stringing concertina wire, enduring endless artillery bombardments, marching into machine guns, fighting hand-to-hand and killing up close, the homeroom class is shot, shelled, and blasted apart. The horror is relieved by a few incidents of low comedy, dalliance, and an uncomfortable home leave, but the rule is inexorable and inevitable death: files of pack-laden troops mowed down by withering machine gun fire; the noise, smoke, and chaos of forward assault; the lunar landscape of the no-man's-land. As Armistice negotiations drag on, the hero (Lew Ayres)—or rather protagonist—is killed by a sniper while reaching over the parapets to touch a butterfly. A double exposure reprises the earnest young faces marching off to war over another kind of no-man's-land, a graveyard filled with white crosses, row on row. . . .

Doom and Gloom

The doom of the battlefield and the gloom of the homefront were the dominant shadings until the very eve of the Second World War. Hollywood conjured a few frivolous and glorious marches off to war, such as the alternately zany and grim *What Price Glory?* (1926) and, on the eve of a mythic turnabout, the Hibernian frolic *The Fighting 69th* (1940). Unlike Europeans, the relatively unscathed Americans might sustain a portion of the grand illusion. More often, though, whether in *The Lost Patrol* (1934) or *The Dawn Patrol* (both the 1930 original and the 1938 remake), men at war were wiped out one by one. MGM's *They Gave Him a Gun* (1937) occupies the center of gravity. A product of the most glamorous and politically conservative of the studios, it opens with a merchants-of-death montage tracing the manufacture of a firearm in a humming munitions factory. . . . The film charts the progress of a peaceful hayseed turned into a trained killer by the U.S. military. Urged to bayonet the abdomen of a dummy by his bloodthirsty drill sergeant, the raw recruit faints dead away, but soon he itches to get off the target range and demonstrate his sharpshooting skills on flesh and blood. In battle he passes his test, picking off a German machine gun crew one by one, including a soldier who raises his arms in surrender. Stateside, he puts his expertise to work as a gangster until he is hunted down and killed in a hail of civilian bullets. His former drill sergeant, now a police sergeant, moans that "this was one of my boys." "He was your star pupil," spits out an embittered pal. As late as 1939, a *March of Time* retrospective on Hollywood history matter-of-factly referred to *All Quiet on the Western Front* as the "greatest of war pictures." By definition, war movies were antiwar movies.

EXAMINING POP CULTURE

World War II: American Culture Embraces the Allied War Effort

Hollywood's Contributions to the War Effort

Allen L. Woll

In the late 1930s, as the Nazi threat grew, Hollywood abandoned the pacifist stance it had adopted in the 1920s and instead produced several films that advocated, either directly or indirectly, U.S. entry into World War II. A new genre of films (now known simply as World War II films) began to feature pro-military and anti-Nazi themes. At first these films were met with controversy, because many Americans believed that America should stay out of what they viewed as a European conflict. However, after the Japanese bombing of Pearl Harbor in 1941, these isolationist sentiments all but disappeared.

Allen L. Woll explains in this excerpt from his book *The Hollywood Musical Goes to War* that after Pearl Harbor the U.S. government embraced Hollywood as a valuable partner in the war effort. In 1943 the U.S. government formed the Office of War Information (OWI), which to some degree regulated Hollywood's portrayal of the war. The OWI monitored film plots that dealt with sensitive subjects, such as America's relationship with Russia, and urged filmmakers to emphasize the teamwork, sacrifice, and commitment that would be required for victory.

HOLLYWOOD ENTERED THE SECOND WORLD
War almost three years before Washington, D.C. While the

■

Excerpted from *The Hollywood Musical Goes to War*, by Allen L. Woll. © 1983 by Allen L. Woll. Reprinted by permission of Burnham Inc., Publishers.

nation wavered between a sympathy for our European friends and a mistrust of outright intervention, film studios released a "flock of features to whip up enthusiasm for preparedness and the draft." *Variety*, the show business oracle, noted the trend almost immediately and dubbed the new films "preparedness pix." By the end of 1940 film schedules were hastily revised to include thirty-six titles concerning "conscription, flying, and other phases of war and defense." With such films as *I Married a Nazi*, *Sergeant York*, and *British Intelligence*, Hollywood assumed an interventionist stance.

Interventionist Filmmakers vs. Isolationist Congressmen

Hollywood's definitive commitment to the European war was looked on less fondly in the halls of Congress where isolationist forces, led by Senator Gerald Nye of North Dakota, had not yet been stilled. The so-called patriotism of Hollywood war films became mere propaganda in the eyes of those legislators who believed that the United States should avoid the terrors of war and leave European nations to fight their own battles. As a result, a subcommittee of the Interstate Commerce Commission met in September, 1941, to investigate "Motion Picture Screen and Radio Propaganda."

This investigation reflected Washington's long-standing distrust of the cinematic medium. The preponderant influence of the motion pictures in matters of morals had long been recognized, but not until the 1930s had fears erupted concerning the political uses of film. The Roosevelt Administration's use of the documentary film to support such projects as the Tennessee Valley Authority angered Congressional opponents who began to understand the political implications of the cinema. By 1941 these initial fears escalated to anger as the hearings swiftly revealed.

Senator Nye, the Committee's second witness, saw the presence of a vast conspiracy urging American entry into the war. Nye contended that screen propaganda was the most insidious of all: "Arriving at the theatre, Mr. and Mrs. America sit, with guard completely down, mind open, ready and eager for entertainment. In that frame of mind they follow through the story which the screen tells. If, somewhere in that story

there is planted a narrative, a speech, or a declaration by a favorite actor or actress which seems to pertain to causes which
are upsetting so much of the world today, there is planted in
the heart and in the mind a feeling, a sympathy, or a distress
which is not easily eliminated." He added that the public knew
and expected propaganda from newspapers, but motion pictures took the audience completely by surprise. Nye placed
blame for this mysterious conspiracy on Jewish interventionist
interests. Although the Senator prefaced his comments with a
perfunctory "some of my best friends are Jews," he repeatedly
criticized Jewish radio commentators, columnists, and publishers for their attempt to deceive the American people.

Senator Bennett C. Clark of Missouri agreed with his col-
league's charges, and specifically condemned the film industry
for the dissemination of interventionist propaganda. He contended that "not one word on the side of the argument against
the war is heard." This was due to the "fact that the moving
picture industry is a monopoly controlled by a half dozen men
dominated by hatred, who are determined in order to wreak
vengeance on Adolf Hitler, a ferocious beast, to plunge this nation into war on behalf of another ferocious beast." Clark's list
of those in charge of the film media included Nicholas
Schenck, Darryl F. Zanuck, Alexander Korda, and Henry Luce,
who was responsible for the "March of Time" series, which
"poisons the minds of the American people to go to war.". . .

Hollywood Is Vindicated by Pearl Harbor

Darryl F. Zanuck, then vice-president in charge of production
at Twentieth Century-Fox, followed Warner on the witness
stand. He detailed his Methodist background in Wahoo, Ne-
braska, (population 891) and recounted his adventures in the
U.S. Army during World War I, where he rose to the rank of
private first class. His testimony followed that of Warner's
fairly closely. Zanuck explained: "In the time of acute national
peril, I feel that it is the duty of every American to give his
complete cooperation and support to our President and our
Congress to do everything to defeat Hitler and preserve
America. If this course of necessity leads to war, I want to follow my President along that course."

Zanuck's testimony met with stirring applause from the

Senate audience, as he explained that pictures are so "strong and powerful that they sold the American way of life, not only to America, but to the entire world. They sold it so strongly that when dictators took over Italy and Germany, what did Hitler and his flunky, Mussolini, do? The first thing they did was to ban our pictures, throw us out. They wanted no part of the American way of life."

The Committee moved to recess after testimony from Barney Balaban, president of Paramount Pictures. The Committee never resumed its meetings. A small column in the *New York Times* announced its demise, since, after the bombing of Pearl Harbor, the isolationist position swiftly dissolved. America entered the war, and Hollywood was now able to use all the facilities at its disposal to help America win the war.

Propaganda or Patriotism?

There seemed to be no way that Warner, Zanuck, or Schenck could deny that Hollywood had been producing films encouraging American entry into the war since early 1939. Whether it was propaganda seemed questionable to the film moguls. As Zanuck claimed: "I usually find that when someone produces something that you do not like, they call it propaganda." Rather, they argued that they were presenting motion pictures which advocated a particular political position. They reasoned that others, given the rights of free speech, might produce films that supported isolationist ideas. In reality, however, no one did so.

The films which preceded American entry into the war were of two types: the metaphorical and the contemporary. The metaphorical films deliberately avoided the current European conflict. They often looked to history for valid analogies to the present political situation. These motion pictures argued that the American people should learn from the lessons of history that war was often necessary in order to defend democracy and the American way of life.

Metaphorical World War II Films

As a result the camera wandered through time and place to discover parallels of current events. For example, *Juarez* (1939) exalted a nineteenth century Mexican president, because he de-

fended his nation against the dictatorial Napoleon III and supported democracy for Latin American nations. The rhetoric of
the film bordered on the contemporary, causing Frank S. Nu-
gent, critic for the *New York Times*, to note "that it is not at all
difficult to read between the lines."

Perhaps the most popular film of this historical genre was
an excursion into the American past with Howard Hawks'
Sergeant York. Producers had attempted to film the life of this
World War I hero since Jesse Lasky broached the idea in 1919.
After years of negotiations, York finally allowed his biography
to be filmed. Alvin York remained on the set during the entire
filming, and later praised Warners for its historical accuracy.

Despite York's claims of the film's veracity, *Sergeant York*
became yet another motion picture which advocated the taking of arms in the defense of democracy. The young Alvin
York (Gary Cooper) finds religion after a misspent youth. He
reads the Bible diligently, and when drafted, refuses to fight,
since he believes "Thou shall not kill." An army major admires
York's ability with a rifle but cannot understand his reluctance
to support the war. He gives York a *History of the United States*,
so the new recruit can learn what the Founding Fathers and
the great American heroes once fought for. ("Daniel Boone
wanted freedom. That's quite a word, *freedom*.") York retreats
to a mountainside to ponder the major's message. A wind
blows the pages of the Bible open to a quotation fraught with
meaning: "Render therefore to Caesar the things that are Caesar's, and to God the things that are God's." A divine light
shines on York's face, and he realizes that he must fight to preserve America's freedom. York has learned from history and
from the Bible that pacifism is irrelevant when the defense of
freedom is concerned. Warner Brothers hoped that the audience would learn the same lesson.

The Direct Approach

The majority of films of this period avoided the indirect approach and considered contemporary society. Some, such as
Confessions of a Nazi Spy, revealed Nazi activities on the homefront. This factual account starred Edward G. Robinson as the
assiduous American agent who uncovered a vast Nazi spy ring
in the United States. The story itself was lifted from trial

records, as well as a series of the *New York Post* articles written by Leon G. Turrou, a former F.B.I. investigator.

Other films concerned German society and the rise of the Nazi party. These films lacked the gritty reality of *Confessions of a Nazi Spy*, but attempted to fictionalize the horrors of Hitler's Germany. *The Mortal Storm* (1941) is typical of this genre. The family of Professor Roth (Frank Morgan) is brutally destroyed as Nazi power is concentrated. Roth's daughter, Freya, (Margaret Sullavan) defends the ideals of freedom, while the male children actively support the Nazi cause. Professor Roth, an anatomist, is ousted from the university because he refuses to support theories of Aryan superiority. He is

Nostalgia for "The Good War"

Every year to date continues to see the release of one or more major World War II movie productions. The propaganda may not be quite so blatant but the flag is still waving, and no doubt exists about who is good and who is bad. Nothing has daunted the American movie audience response to World War II film stories—not even other conflicts and armed hostilities. In fact, the reverse has been true. New battles send Hollywood and moviegoers back to Good War films.

The conflict in Korea increased the production of World War II films, and the 1970 release of *Patton* at the height of the Vietnam War proved that the American public's love affair with the Good War was in little danger of being ended by other genres. *Patton* was a tremendous success at the box office as well as an Oscar winner for Best Picture, Best Director, and Best Actor (George C. Scott). Even President Nixon openly admitted that it was his favorite film, and it was rumored that he rewatched the movie before making difficult decisions about the war in Southeast Asia.

Patton opens with Scott, in full dress uniform, delivering a speech which Patton himself presented to his troops

then arrested and sent to a concentration camp. Roth's family attempts to emigrate, but Freya is detained. She eventually attempts to flee through the Austrian mountains with her lover, a young idealist, portrayed by James Stewart, but she is shot by Nazi troops led by her former boyfriend (Robert Young).

Four Sons, I Married a Nazi, and *So Ends Our Night* also followed this pattern of the breaking of family ties in the face of the Nazi menace. Other films which considered Germany were primarily of the espionage type (*Man Hunt, Underground*), but they maintained a firm anti-Nazi position.

What remained a minor trend before American entry into the war, soon became a torrent after Pearl Harbor. No longer

during the war. In a scene direct from 1940s Hollywood, and one that could be included in any Good War film (with the possible exception of the profanity), Scott/Patton states, "Be seated. Now, I want you to remember that no bastard ever won a war by dying for his country. He won it by making the other poor bastard die for his country. Men, all the stuff you heard about America not wanting to fight, wanting to stay out of the war, is a lot of horse dung. Americans, traditionally, love to fight. All real Americans love the sting of battle. When you were kids, you all admired the champion marble shooter, the fastest runner, the big-league ballplayer, the toughest boxer. Americans love a winner and will not tolerate a loser. Americans play to win all the time. I wouldn't give a hoot in hell for a man who lost and laughed. That's why Americans have never lost—and will never lose—a war, because the very thought of losing is hateful to Americans."

American films about the Good War continue time and time again to reinforce Patton's sentiments. Unfortunately, somewhere along the way Americans and the movies lost sight of the possibility that things would not always be as Patton predicted.

Michael Lee Lanning, *Vietnam at the Movies,* 1994.

was there any attempt to limit films opposed to Nazi Germany or those praising American ideals. In the next four years, Hollywood produced countless films which attempted to win the war in the hearts and minds of American citizens.

Hollywood at War

Life changed behind the screen as well. The active support of Washington's war policy was not only evident in the finished film product. Producers, directors, stars, extras, musicians, electricians, and carpenters gave more to the war effort than motion pictures. Hollywood's nightlife collapsed, and many restaurants remained open only on weekends. The carefree life of the previous decade dimmed considerably as the denizens of the film capital flocked to assist the war effort.

Volunteer organizations flourished shortly after Pearl Harbor. Stars joined every possible committee: the Volunteer Army Canteen Service, Bundles for Bluejackets, the Aerial Nurse Corps, the Women's Ambulance Defense Corps, and the Civil Air Patrol. They even became air raid spotters and wardens.

More than five hundred actors joined the Actors' Committee of the Hollywood Victory Committee for Stage, Screen, and Radio. This organization, headed by Clark Gable, arranged benefit performances for the Red Cross, Navy Relief Fund, and other wartime organizations. Others began crosscountry tours to sell defense bonds. Carole Lombard was killed on one of these trips. Dorothy Lamour, known as the "Sweetheart of the Treasury," completed Lombard's itinerary and travelled more than ten thousand miles on visits to defense plants and shipyards.

Even film studios volunteered their services. The most noteworthy of these efforts was the contribution of half of the Walt Disney studios for films concerning defense projects. Donald Duck and Mickey Mouse thus appeared gratis in films for the Treasury Department and the Office of Inter-American Affairs.

General Lewis Hershey declared that the film industry was "essential" during wartime. As a result, he allowed studios to apply for draft deferments for irreplaceable workers. Despite the government's permission for major stars, directors, and writers to remain safely in Hollywood, many luminaries decided to enlist. Frank Capra, John Ford, Garson Kanin,

William Wyler, and Darryl Zanuck offered their film-making talents to the War Department.

Actors also joined the exodus. Clark Gable departed soon after the death of his wife, Carole Lombard. James Stewart gained ten pounds so he could pass the physical and become a private. The numbers of leading men that deserted Hollywood during the war led to a crisis, as capable male actors became impossible to find for many new films.

The Office of War Information

In this fashion, Hollywood became a major ally to Washington. While the film capital was seen as an antagonist in the days before Pearl Harbor, government advisors began to realize that the film industry could be of major help in the war effort. Leo Rosten, the novelist and a deputy director of the Office of War Information (OWI), explained the value of the motion picture to the American audience:

> The movies can give the public information. But they can do more than that; they can give the public understanding. They can clarify problems that are complex and confusing. They can focus attention upon the key problems which the people must decide, the basic choices which people make. They can make clear and intelligible the enormous complexities of global geography, military tactics, economic dilemmas, political disputes, and psychological warfare. The singularly illuminating tools of the screen can be used to give the people a clear, continuous, and comprehensible picture of the total pattern of total war.

The motion picture seemed the ideal medium to fulfill OWI goals. Established in June 1942 by executive order, the OWI was designed to "disseminate war information" and facilitate the understanding of the "policies, activities, and aims of the Government" during World War II. Motion pictures could therefore play a vital role in this effort.

Despite Hollywood's willingness to help on a voluntary basis, it was no secret that the leaders of the film industry feared the imposition of government censorship. They were somewhat surprised when Lowell Mellett, head of the Bureau of Motion Pictures (BMP) of the OWI, explained to an audience of film producers that he was "hoping that most of you and your fellow workers would stay right here in Hollywood and keep on doing what you're doing, because your motion pictures are a vital contribution to the total defense effort." At first this statement bewildered the assembled film producers. When one asked Mellett if the industry should make "hate pictures," Mellett replied, "Use your own judgment. We'll give you our advice if you want us to."

Yet, the OWI was not going to sit passively on the sidelines. Mellett explained that his office would fulfill two functions. First, he would attempt to advise Hollywood about Washington's attitudes concerning future films. Producers could submit their ideas voluntarily to his office, which would then determine proper policy after discussion with the State Department. In this manner film plots concerning Russia or China, for example, would follow official foreign policy decisions. Despite Mellett's calming tone, the fine line between advice and censorship was often cloudy. Within a short time, Mellett's office would be perceived as the enemy as it began to insist that both scripts and dialogue be changed to suit the needs of the government.

"Us vs. Them" in World War II Films

Ralph Willett

In the following essay American Studies professor
Ralph Willett explores how World War II was portrayed in popular films throughout the 1940s. For the
most part these films applaud the war effort while also
showing a minimal amount of the actual violence the
war entailed. The Nazis are routinely ridiculed, stereotyped, and demonized in films made during the war,
and in films released after the bombing of Pearl Harbor the Japanese are often portrayed as subhuman. In
seeming contradiction to the racist way in which the
enemy is depicted, U.S. combat units in World War II
films are often multiracial, in accordance with the Office of War Information's (OWI) recommendation that
Hollywood stress America's national unity.

IT WAS NOT ONLY DURING THE ACTUAL WAR
years that the American film glorified the war effort and
shaped the nation's attitudes towards foreign tyranny. By 1939
Confessions of a Nazi Spy (which identified a spy ring within the
German-American Bund) was already directing attention to
the infiltration of fascist ideology. The following year saw
Hollywood using a European setting for anti-Nazi propaganda in such films as *The Mortal Storm* and *Four Sons*. It was
at this time that the American cinema began to stereotype
German soldiers and agents as efficient, even ruthless men,
who were also suave and decadently self-indulgent in their
taste for luxury, good food and wine, and culture. Germany's

■

Excerpted from Ralph Willett, "The Nation in Crisis: Hollywood's Response to the
1940s," © Ralph Willett, in *Cinema, Politics, and Society in America*, edited by Philip
Davies and Brian Neve. Copyright © 1981 Manchester University Press. Reprinted
by permission of the author.

military leaders, however, while being presented as dangerous gangsters, were also caricatured as absurd, ridiculous creatures, an approach for which Chaplin (with *The Great Dictator* in 1940) must bear some of the responsibility, and one which he later regretted. But since dictatorship was, to Americans, anachronistic, it was a natural impulse to laugh at its practitioners, and *The Great Dictator* was at least unambiguous in its anti-Nazi feeling.

Contemporary Europe, which had been relatively neglected during the Depression, was being re-created by American directors, a number of whom were exiles from Germany itself. They assisted in the internalization of the old European-American opposition; while the German fascists lived in sumptuous, over-decorated apartments, the 'democratic' resistance fighters lived in mean cottages and plotted in cellars. Nazi officers, though sometimes portrayed by European exiles, were frequently played by English actors (George Sanders, Cedric Hardwicke) with upper-class accents; on the other hand, it was not unusual to hear American intonations in a 'European' village.

By 1940 European events had created a need in America for didactic newsreels, which made defence preparations, in the diluted form of parades and meetings, acceptable, even enjoyable. The reality of armed conflict was avoided; instead of death and mutilation, military leaders and troops in transit were featured. Further techniques employed were the mixture of documentary, instructional and fictional material in the propaganda series *Why We Fight* made from 1942 to 1945, and the use of a hortatory speech in the last reel to promote American readiness to join the war and to hasten rearmament. Hitchcock's *Foreign Correspondent* (1940), for example, ends with an impassioned radio broadcast from London: 'The lights are going out in Europe. Ring yourself around with steel, America.' Less successful, though, was the revival of *All Quiet on the Western Front* (1930) in 1941; the futility and horror of war and the stark images of dying men emerged too strongly.

Glorifying War and Democracy

Although in 1941 a Senate committee objected to Hollywood's anti-Nazi pictures, the Selective Service Act had been passed in the previous year; and after Pearl Harbor, the alliance between the American film industry and the American government became complete, with the authorities even suggesting particular themes that Hollywood should exploit. The Bureau of Motion Pictures, part of OWI, increased its influence over scripts and films especially during and after 1943 when the censorial Ulric Bell took over the Hollywood office. Hollywood, on the whole, responded compliantly, and it is hardly surprising that, under these circumstances, the movies produced were simplistic melodramas, glorifying war and democracy (the 'civilised' nations), while vilifying the enemy as the representatives of barbarism. Even in 1944 James Agee, writing regularly in the *Nation*, was obliged, repeatedly, to call attention to the different levels of reality attained in Hollywood war fictions and English documentaries. The latter, he remarked, avoided the American disease of 'masked contempt and propitiation', and throughout his essays he persistently notes the absurdities and distortions perpetrated by the standard Hollywood product. The tendency to portray the inhabitants of Occupied Europe patronisingly, as foreign versions of folksy Middle Americans, has already been mentioned; Agee singled out the pro-Russian *Mission to Moscow* (1943), a thoroughly inaccurate film made by Warners with Roosevelt's approval, as a particularly blatant example of despising the American audience: 'there is no essential difference, it turns out, between the Soviet Union and the good old USA, except that in Russia everybody affects an accent and women run locomotives'. In that film, and others like it (*The North Star*, 1943), the Russians, who sing folksongs but use cosmetics, are friendly, hard-working and heroic, while communism is an Eastern version of the New Deal. Such pro-Soviet attitudes later produced accusations and bitterness during the Cold War.

Equally false, Agee pointed out, was the bromidic treatment of death. Dying was not only sanctioned by patriotism but it was usually presented without a sense of horror or revulsion. Heaven and Hell were frequently depicted in 1940s movies, though neither these 'locations' nor their inhabitants were in any way disturbing. The majority of ghosts were pleasant, even charming, while in such films as *All That Money Can Buy* (1941) and *Heaven Can Wait* (1943) even the Devil (played by Laird Cregar) was made inoffensive and rather attractive.

The Propagandist Machine

Films which gave a true picture of combat conditions or of the psychological effects of war received short shrift from the Pentagon, with John Huston becoming the chief victim of official suppression. *Let There Be Light* (1945), which set out to show that the emotional casualties of war were neither lunatics nor social misfits, was banned, while *The Battle of San Pietro* (1944), which graphically depicted Americans in the Italian campaign being shot or burnt to death, was not allowed to reach the

Demonizing the Enemy

American filmmakers adopted several other methods besides name-calling in their campaign of derision against the Axis powers. . . .

The Japanese, and especially the Germans, are often shown thoughtlessly killing their own soldiers if it serves their purposes. Enemy riflemen and especially fighter pilots are shown grinning with delight and sometimes laughing as they gun down Americans, who are sometimes unarmed.

These films include references to Germans and especially the Japanese as cruel and barbaric, preying mostly upon the weak. Germans and Japanese are shown to be capable of bloody and needless reprisals against civilians, including rape, and the murder of women and children.

By the end of the war the Allies were almost as guilty as the Axis powers when it came to bombing civilians (more so, if we count Hiroshima and Nagasaki)—although Americans were always shown in our films bombing just military targets, and then only in so-called "surgical strikes." But the enemy was repeatedly shown taking great pains to bomb civilian targets, especially orphanages, schools, churches, and hospitals. . . .

The differences between "us"—and "them"—were made clear in movie after movie during the war. These differences included the Japanese disregard for human life and

public. The truthful rendering of the sufferings of American soldiers in war was of little or no value to the propagandist machine. Reality needed to be manipulated rather than shown objectively, in order to intensify hatred of the enemy. Japanese soldiers, played by Chinese-American actors, were typed as subhuman animals, pitiless and, above all, sadistic in a continuation of popular culture racism; and into this psychological climate, Hollywood could inject an atrocity picture, *The Purple Heart* (1944), based on what were then unverified facts,

liberty and their godlike worship of their emperor. Hollywood also showed us the Germans' love of totalitarianism, their plans to make all other nations slaves of the Third Reich, and their worshipful devotion to Hitler. As an example of their imperialistic aims, in *Casablanca* Vichy Captain Renault greets SS Major Strasser as he arrives in the North African city. Renault apologizes for the oppressive heat, but Strasser dismisses Renault's concern, saying that Germans (because of their conquests) must become accustomed to all climates.

In these films, gangster-like behavior was standard for the Germans and frequent for the Japanese, especially in spy films such as *Across The Pacific*. This of course included thievery, the classic double-cross, and officers whose word (including the white flag of truce) could not be trusted. For example, during a lull in the battle between a small band of allied soldiers preventing a battalion of Germans from occupying an oasis in *Sahara*, a swinish Nazi colonel orders his troops to open fire on an allied soldier who waves a white flag while returning to the Allied trenches.

Finally, American film propagandists took great pains to remind us of the Japanese and German disdain for the Allies. In particular, films displayed sneering German and Japanese officers voicing their disdain for American virtue, religion, rule of law, and freedom.

Ralph R. Donald, "Savages, Swine & Buffoons," *Images Journal*, May 1999.

with impunity. The army's *Screen Magazine* referred to the Japanese as 'rats' and 'cockroaches', and even *Guadalcanal Diary* (1943) more acceptable for its realism, contains its share of racist references: 'Where's the rest of the seven dwarfs?' 'They live in the trees like apes.'

Guadalcanal Diary is typical of the best and the worst of the American war film. It does show men wounded and shell-shocked, 'old before their time', and it does admit the omnipresence of fear: 'Anyone who says he isn't scared', says the sergeant, 'is either a fool or a liar.' Moreover, the class distinctions that were to bedevil English war films well into the 1950s are conspicuously absent. However, the 'realistic' shots are always brief; the question of the morality of war, of 'killing *people*' is abruptly settled by the sergeant: 'Besides, they're not people', he says of the Japanese; and the Brooklyn taxi-driver's mild protest against war ('I don't like it') tails off in pious fatalism ('I guess it's up to God'). War is inevitable, so there is no examination of the forces and pressures that create wars.

The Melting Pot in World War II Films

The formula element in the film lies not only in its attitude towards the Japanese, but in the multi-racial composition of the marine company: a Jew, a Mexican, a black American and a variety of WASP American types. This was the 1940s variation of the 'Pro-assimilative' process observable in 1930s films, encouraged by the OWI's *Government Information Manual for the Motion Picture* (1942), which recommended, among other measures, the use of 'colored' soldiers and servicemen with foreign names as a way of stressing national unity. Pictures of racial integration might help to allay racial tensions at home. Moreover, the emphasis on ethnicity offered an occasion for racial pride, while at the same time reassuring ethnic minorities that by participating in this communal enterprise they were demonstrating their 'Americanness', their shared values of freedom, patriotism, home and the family.

Popular Culture Mobilizes for the War Effort

Michael Renov

The American war effort in World War II involved far more than just the military. Women and men on the homefront supported the soldiers abroad with their labor and their spirit. Their patriotic fervor was echoed in all facets of the popular culture of the era. Popular music incorporated military and patriotic themes. Many of the best-selling books of the period were first-hand accounts of the war experience, from the point of view of both the soldiers on active duty and the women on the homefront. The public developed a voracious appetite for news about the war, and magazine publishing and radio broadcasting flourished. Finally, the advertising industry was transformed as it worked with the Office of War Information to promote scrap drives, rationing, and war bonds.

   Michael Renov is a professor of critical studies in the School of Cinema-Television at the University of Southern California and author of *Hollywood's Wartime Woman: Representation and Ideology*, from which the following is excerpted.

EVERY FORM OF ENTERTAINMENT OR COMMUNI-cation was touched by the war and the rapid alterations of social patterns. Popular songs were, as ever, a kind of barometer of contemporary experience with the favorite tunes offering a

■

rough chronology of the emotional tides of the day—the sorrow of parting ("I'll Wait for You," "I'll Never Smile Again"), the giddiness of rapid change ("Boogie-Woogie Bugle Boy," "GI Jive"), the blend of nostalgia and postwar optimism ("White Christmas"). But unlike World War I, with its rousing anthem "Over There," tunesmiths were unable to galvanize the emotions of the days after Pearl Harbor into a single, rallying song, although they did their best with such forgettable efforts as "Goodbye, Momma, I'm Off to Yokohama," "Slap the Jap Right off the Map" and "To Be Specific, It's Our Pacific."

Many songs, written under the aegis of the Songwriters' War Committee, expressed clearly propagandistic aims. "Fighting on the Home Front *WINS*" was tagged as the "official war song of the American housewife." Other female-oriented tunes were "The Woman behind the Man behind the Gun," "We're the Janes Who Make the Planes," "We Build 'em, You Sail 'em" and "Rosie the Riveter." While many a bawdy ditty celebrated the soldier's romantic exploits ("Dirtie Gertie from Bizerte"), the girl he left behind was left holding the double standard. It was rare that a song suggested her infidelity except in the most humorous vein ("You Can't Say No to a Soldier," "I'm Doin' It for Defense"). More likely she was depicted as the loyal and lonely girl of the GI's dream, as in "Don't Get around Much Anymore" and "Saturday Night Is the Loneliest Night of the Week." These songs, although aimed at the largely female home front audience, express the male wish and point-of-view, thus constituting one example among many of the manner in which the ideological regime (in this case, identifiably patriarchal) shapes and produces popular culture.

News and Funnies

The war created an insatiable demand for news coverage; the newspaper industry responded with aggressive coverage on every front. The newspaper business underwent the same kind of consolidation and growth evidenced elsewhere in the economy: fewer newspapers survived the war, while overall circulation rose dramatically. The sheer volume of reportage was unprecedented, with four hundred and fifty newspaper correspondents covering the landing on Normandy Beach on D-Day.

While many of the most celebrated writers of fiction lay down the pen for more active war participation ([author] Theodore Dreiser's comment is indicative of the trend: "Only a slacker would set about writing a novel when there were so many cartridges to be milled and ditches to be dug"), the purveyors of the comic art were not similarly inclined. It was estimated that forty million readers each day followed the exploits of a blond prizefighter named Joe Palooka as he enlisted into the service. Most of the other top-rated strips ("Blondie," "Li'l Abner," "Li'l Orphan Annie") chose to avoid direct participation in the war with the philosophy (based upon their mailbags) that the GIs wanted to maintain a connection to home and to peacetime. Several of the women's strips took a different tack. Although "Dixie Dugan" (the source of a war-oriented 20th Century-Fox comedy in 1942) remained a hare-brained heroine, "Winnie Winkle" married a soldier and "Tillie the Toiler" joined the WAC [Women's Army Corps].

Popular Literature

The literary fortunes of war generally favored nonfiction over fiction, with first-person accounts of war remaining popular. The nonfictional bestsellers, although diverse in tone and intention, shared a common interest in the world beyond our borders: William L. Shirer's *Berlin Diary*, ex-Soviet Ambassador Joseph Davies' *Mission to Moscow* (later to become a Warner Brothers production), Private Marion Hargrove's overnight comic bestseller *See Here, Private Hargrove* (also sold to Hollywood) and the surprise hit by 1940s Republican presidential candidate, Wendell Willkie, *One World*, which was the top-selling book in America for sixteen consecutive weeks in 1943. A major trend in popular fiction was the religious epic, as exemplified by Lloyd Douglas's *The Robe* and Franz Werfel's *The Song of Bernadette*. John Steinbeck was the only major novelist to write a bona fide war novel, *The Moon Is Down*, which, like its film adaptation, was received with mixed reviews owing to its unwillingness to portray its major German character as a full-fledged villain. John Hersey emerged as a promising young writer with three war novels, the last of which, *A Bell for Adano*, was awarded the Pulitzer Prize. There were several popular novels authored by women, among them Pearl Buck's

Dragon Seed, Betty Smith's *A Tree Grows in Brooklyn*, and Kathleen Winsor's *Forever Amber*.

But the real wartime story of women's literature was the emergence of a new genre of writing based upon first-hand experiences in war factories or observations on the burgeoning opportunities and responsibilities of the American woman. Many were humorous: Constance Bowman's *Slacks and Callouses*, Nell Giles' *Punch In, Susie!: A Woman's War Factory Diary*, or Elizabeth Hawes's *Why Women Cry or Wenches with Wrenches*. Others took a more serious but equally personal approach often adopting a first-person narrative style, e.g., Mable Gerken's *Ladies in Pants: A Home Front Diary*, Augusta H. Clawson's *Shipyard Diary of a Woman Welder*, and Margaret Buell Wilder's *Since You Went Away . . . Letters to a Soldier from His Wife* (quickly bought and adapted to the screen by David O. Selznick). A related cycle of books appeared which were guides to the bewildering new world of war jobs and were more directly informational: *Women in War Industry: The Complete Guide to a War Factory Job*, by Laura Nelson Baker; *Arms and the Girl: A Guide to Personal Adjustment in War Work and War Marriage*, by Gulielma Fell Alsop and Mary F. McBride; and Evelyn M. Steele's *Wartime Opportunities for Women*. This flood of women's literature was one manifestation of the exhilaration and creative energy which the war years helped unleash in the American female population.

The war was a boom period for the magazine industry. With the War Production Board's mandated allotment of 75 percent of prewar paper tonnage, it became increasingly difficult to find copies of the most popular magazines. This was the heyday of photojournalism with the pages of *Life* and *Look* bringing the war theaters to the home front each week. The most popular American magazines began to be exported worldwide and joined the motion pictures as major purveyors of the American way of life to the world. A change in the women's magazine market paralleled the rise of women's fiction. With women a growing percentage of the reading audience, several magazines were founded which were aimed at the younger, newly affluent readership: *Mademoiselle*, *Glamour* and *Seventeen*, all of which remained fixtures of the industry. Clearly, the altered profile of the American woman was having a profound effect upon marketing strategies within the publishing industry.

The Golden Period of Radio

World War II was the golden period of radio. Broadcast income rose 125 percent from 1942 to 1944. The higher rates of taxation convinced many corporations to advertise rather than turn over huge amounts of their capital to Uncle Sam. This fact, coupled with newsprint shortages which resulted in a lack of advertising space, made radio the windfall recipient of extensive sponsorship. Businesses and major corporations stood in line to sponsor prime-time programming. The major formats were detective/mystery dramas, which often involved war themes, comedy/variety shows, and, of course, news programs. The medium was deeply involved in the war effort. The Office of War Information allocated pertinent subjects to be discussed during serious curtain talks on each comedy show. Many comics including Bob Hope took their shows on the road, broadcasting from military bases and hospitals around the world. And, of course, radio stars such as Hope, Fred Allen, Eddie Cantor and Edgar Bergen played an active role in the series of war bond campaigns that were helping to finance the war.

As for radio advertising, early evidence of bad taste was particularly apparent by its juxtaposition with serious war coverage. A broadcast from a war zone was likely to be interrupted by a message from a sponsor saying, "Here is a late important news bulletin. Use Smith Brothers Cough Drops," or "Use Gillette Blades which last longer, and thereby conserve steel for national defense." Stations and even networks began to ban this kind of crass and exploitive commercialism.

As was the case with the newspaper industry, the backbone of radio during this period was hard news; CBS estimated that war coverage comprised more than one-third of its total program hours from Pearl Harbor to V-E Day. Many news personalities who were to achieve prominence in the yet-to-be-born television industry captured public attention through their on-the-scenes broadcasts from war fronts. Edward R. Murrow gave listeners a first-hand description of the bombing of Berlin in a radio first. Eric Sevareid bailed out over the Burmese jungle and lived to tell Americans about it.

The major radio networks donated time and costs for the broadcast of a wartime morale series, "This Is War," which was carried simultaneously by 550 stations. In a manner similar to the motion picture industry, the radio networks donated countless hours of commercial programming for broadcast by the Armed Services Radio Service. The single biggest radio event of the war years was the coverage of the death of FDR, who had been the first president to include radio correspondents in White House press conferences and had used the medium most cannily in his Fireside Chats; Roosevelt's death was broadcast to the nation one minute after it was announced at the White House on April 12, 1945. For the next three days all commercial advertising was cancelled during the coverage of the funeral procession from Warm Springs, Georgia to Washington to Hyde Park.

The War Advertising Council

The last facet of popular culture to be discussed, while rarely considered to be an area of artistic production, played a particularly crucial role during the war years. The American advertising industry provided much of the leadership in the mounting of government strategy for the management of the war on the home front. From the outset of hostilities, it was clear that the newly appointed agency heads in Washington, most coming directly from business and industry, favored the promotion of governmental programs through campaigns modeled on commercial advertising techniques. Furthermore, the mass media—newspapers, magazines, radio and motion pictures— were instantly recognized as the key instruments of state policy. Early in the war a group of advertising executives formed the War Advertising Council (the WAC acronym was exceedingly popular, designating at once a female branch of the armed services, the film industry's War Activities Committee, and the Women's Advisory Committee to the War Manpower Commission), which helped to coordinate the various campaigns from Washington while persuading thousands of firms and individuals to donate advertising space, time, and talent.

Within government agencies there was a decided split between those favoring the talents of writers and journalists in the promotion of war programs (scrap drives, man- and womanpower campaigns, bond drives) versus those who supported the use of more commercially oriented writers, the "soap salesmen" as they were called. The rift and its eventual outcome are represented by the transformation that occurred within the Office of Facts and Figures. Established in October 1941, the agency was headed by Archibald MacLeish, poet and Librarian of Congress, whose sensibility and political concerns rendered him an early and eloquent opponent of Fascism. MacLeish was a believer in the power of the American people to act wisely when given adequate information and a little gentle guidance. "A democratic government," said MacLeish, "is more concerned with the provision of information to the people than it is with the communication of dreams and aspirations. . . . The duty of government is to provide a basis for judgment, and when it goes beyond that, it goes beyond the prime scope of its duty."

"Selling" Patriotism

But a rising tide of opinion favored the view espoused by Harvard psychologist Gordon Alport: "Public relations, advertising and public opinion work are war industries and ought to be mobilized." An executive order in June of 1942 established the Office of War Information from the ashes of the Office of Facts and Figures and was the occasion for MacLeish's departure in favor of Elmer Davis, a newspaperman and radio broadcaster whose straightforward manner and media experience were more appropriate to the new policies of the agency. A key component of the new operation was the utilization and manipulation of the very "dreams and aspirations" eschewed by MacLeish. The door was opened to the dream-peddlers of Madison Avenue, and the OWI, along with other major government agencies, was soon "selling" its ideas to the American public. The outcome of this internal struggle is crucial to an understanding of the tenor of state involvement in the evolution of American wartime culture.

The full cooperation of the advertising industry was chiefly facilitated by a bargain struck with the Treasury Department which, early on, announced that advertising in "reasonable" amounts constituted a legitimate wartime business expense and was therefore tax deductible at a time when soaring tax rates were causing corporate America great distress. With the liveli-hood of its members insured for the duration, in 1942 the War Advertising Council embarked on a series of energetic cam-paigns for eight different government agencies, with that num-ber doubling in 1943 and again in 1944. Under the tutelage of the War Advertising Council, American businesses donated over a billion dollars in print space and broadcast time to pro-mote war aims and government-sponsored drives.

The symbiotic relationship between government and the private sector was nowhere more apparent than in the ad cam-paigns of the many companies whose plants had been con-verted to the manufacture of war products. With profits and taxes sky-high and a generous advertising budget sound busi-ness practice, it was nonetheless impossible for these busi-nesses to promote the familiar peacetime consumer items. Yet it was imperative that these firms maintain high product visi-bility in preparation for the post-war boom of consumerism that lay ahead. The government, lobbying for the donation of "war advertising" by private industry, defined as advertising that "which induces people, through information, understand-ing, and persuasion to take certain actions necessary to the winning of the war." Many of the major manufacturers, disen-franchised by conversion to war production, chose to attach their names or logos to unvarnished promotional pitches for some government-sponsored program or other—a bond or scrap drive, a rationing reminder—thus avowing their patrio-tism and generosity while keeping themselves in the public eye. As a result of such strategies, advertising volume in dol-lars rose dramatically during the war years despite the 25 per-cent reduction in available paper for publishing. Other com-modity-producing concerns adopted a creative approach to war advertising exemplified by a war slogan that sold hats: "Keep It under Your Stetson" (a warning to beware of loose talk that could betray the secrecy of war operations). The cam-paign thus enabled the Stetson Hat Company to enhance the prestige of its commercial operation while promoting a war aim. A particularly noteworthy advertising strategy involved negative incentives for commodity consumption under the pretext of patriotism and public interest. Firms such as BF Goodrich invested in campaigns to encourage the conservation of rubber since "Hitler smiles when you waste miles." Long term goals were being served with the philosophy that such copy would maintain brand name preferences and help to create post-war demand. Whatever the strategy, advertising continued to play a key role in the shaping of the communal beliefs which fueled the fighting on the home front. The tangibles of the American way of life were the cars, the appliances, the homes that the soldiers were defending and to which they hoped to return. The linkage of consumerism and patriotism, although temporarily reversed ("the good citizen learns to conserve"), was preparing the way for new levels of peacetime business prosperity that would wipe out the memory of the depression years.

Patriotism in World War II Comic Books

William W. Savage Jr.

Much of the popular culture in the 1930s was escapist—rather than addressing current social issues, much of popular entertainment was intended to take people's minds off the economic hardships caused by the Great Depression. Comic books, which emerged in the late 1930s and featured fantastical heroes and stories, became synonymous with escapist entertainment.

In contrast to the complex and controversial issues surrounding the Great Depression, the outbreak of World War II united Americans in opposition to a common enemy. Comic book publishers seized upon the national mood and created heroes, such as Captain America, that reflected the newfound patriotism. Superhero comics changed their focus from crime-fighting to war stories, but retained their escapist nature. Allied heroes and Axis villains were almost always portrayed in black and white terms, and the stories still featured many fantastical elements. War comics were very popular among active-duty soldiers and may have played an important role in keeping up morale. And the popularity of war comics among traditional teen audiences on the home front indicates how eager Americans were for stories that applauded the war effort and glorified U.S. soldiers.

William W. Savage Jr. is a professor of history at the University of Oklahoma. The following selection

■

Excerpted from *Commies, Cowboys, and Jungle Queens: Comic Books and America, 1945–1954*, by William W. Savage Jr., paperback edition published by Wesleyan University Press, 1998. Originally published as *Comic Books and America, 1945–1954*; © 1990 by the University of Oklahoma Press. Reprinted by permission of Wesleyan University Press.

is from his 1990 book *Comic Books and America, 1945–1954.*

DURING THE 1930S, PURVEYORS OF POPULAR CUL-
ture offered escape to the American people. Perhaps they were simply trying to ease Americans through a difficult time by making no offensive reference to the extent of economic calamity wrought by the Depression. If so, the tactic led them conveniently away from the arena of social commentary and thus from the taint of controversy. Concern over Communist activity (the legacy of the Red Scare of the 1920s), distrust of some labor unions, and reaction to even the vaguest of utterances suggestive of socialist sentiment in response to the perceived collapse of capitalism—easy enough to imagine in the 1930s—had all worked toward the kind of consensus that made most social (and necessarily, political and economic) criticism suspect. So, whether the Depression was too dangerous to contemplate or merely too unpleasant, popular culture tended to focus on either the past or the future. Rarely did it examine the present in any relevant manner. . . .

The Origins of Comic Books

On January, 7, 1929, the adventures of "Tarzan" and "Buck Rogers" first appeared on newspaper comic pages, heralding the advent of what would become known as the "adventure strip." Following "Tarzan" in the 1930s were "Dick Tracy," "Jungle Jim," "The Phantom," "Terry and the Pirates," and dozens of others. All of them featured continuing stories, exotic locales and/or characters, virtually nonstop action, and little if any humor. They served to transport readers elsewhere—to a jungle, a desert, the Far East, a distant planet, or some other atypical environment where heroes struggled against tall odds or fabulous creatures, and where nothing had any real bearing on the problems of the day. As the decade progressed, adventure strips grew in popularity, fueling escapist fantasies for the economically distressed. Because comic books developed from comic strips, they reflected the same shifting emphases.

The comic book emerged as a discrete medium of American cultural expression early in the 1930s. In its initial form, it contained only reprints of newspaper comic strips and was offered by publishers in bulk to companies in search of premiums and giveaways to increase their sales of everything from breakfast cereal to children's shoes. So popular was the comic book in this entrepreneurial venue that some publishers were led to believe it could be marketed directly to youngsters through news dealers, drugstores, and other retail outlets for a dime per copy. Early comic books—*Funnies on Parade* (1933) and *Famous Funnies* (1934) were two of the first—bore titles that belied the newspaper trend toward adventure comics, although they did reprint some of the post-1929 adventure strips. But by the end of the decade, such publications as *Detective Comics* (1937) and *Super Comics* (1938) bespoke a significant thematic change, as comic books began to offer more and more original material prepared specifically for the new medium. These items were among the precursors of the vaunted "golden age" of comic books, which began during the summer of 1938 with the debut of Superman in the first issue of *Action Comics*.

The First Superheroes

The impact of the Superman character upon the subsequent development of the comic book would be difficult to overestimate. Here was a seemingly human being who possessed a number of superhuman powers, a costumed hero with a secret identity, an alien from a dying planet who embraced American ideals and Judeo-Christian values—a kind of spectacular immigrant, as it were, come from afar to participate in the American dream. He had speed and strength and was invulnerable to manmade weaponry. He could not fly, but he could jump well enough to sustain the illusion. He was the nemesis of criminals, extracting confessions of their misdeeds by displaying his awesome powers; but, withal, he did not kill, or at least not more than was absolutely necessary—and there was an index of his healthy psyche and wholesome persona. As a cultural artifact, Superman gained an enormous audience in fairly short order, passed from comic books into a variety of media including animated cartoons and radio, and endured in his basic format, though further translated by television and motion pictures, for half a century. If imitation is, as Charles Caleb

Colton said, the most sincere flattery, then Superman was the most flattered of all comic-book creations, spawning a host of look-alike, act-alike costumed heroes, all owing their existence to the norms and conventions his character established.

The appearance of Batman in the May 1939 issue of *Detective Comics* marked the emergence of another kind of heroic prototype. In this instance, a man of means (he had millions), when summoned by police, donned a bizarre costume (intended both to conceal his real identity and to terrify crooks) and swung into action (literally on the end of a rope, in most cases, even though the other end of it did not appear to be attached to anything). Batman possessed no superhuman powers. The skills he offered in behalf of law and order were merely those of the superior athlete and the brilliant scientist, and that was probably as close to reality as the story line came—which is to say that it missed by quite some distance. Like their adversary, Batman's criminal opponents were peculiar characters, altogether unusual in appearance and demeanor; and they contributed much to the surreal, nearly gothic aura of the Batman comic books. . . .

As the 1940s began, comic books were being published in larger and larger quantities, and new characters were appearing every month. Heroes proliferated. The Green Lantern, Captain Marvel, and the Atom led the parade in 1940—respectively, an ordinary mortal endowed with alien powers, a boy who could become a man at will, and an extremely small fellow to whom size, or rather his lack of it, was no handicap in a world of frequently malicious larger folk. By 1941, The Justice Society of America had made its appearance as the first consortium of comic-book heroes: Green Lantern, the Atom, the Flash, Hawkman, Hourman, Sandman, the Spectre, and Dr. Fate collaborated against criminals in a continuing alliance, a unique association that would establish yet another trend within the comic-book industry. Captain America, Plastic Man, Daredevil, and Fighting Yank were among the other heroes who first appeared in 1941. Their very names revealed their unreality. . . .

Comic Books Go to War

All these new heroes had plenty besides crime with which to contend, since, by 1940, war raged in Europe and Japanese militarists were having their way in the Far East. International politics had replaced economics as the major public preoccupation in the United States, and comic-book publishers, seeing fresh opportunities, began paying editorial attention to the real world for the first time. Their heroes, who had been unable to grapple with the complex issues of the Depression, could now set sights on the political arena, at first fighting fascism as a form of international crime in a limited involvement that came several months before America's entry into World War II.

It may have been an appropriate cultural response in the context of the time, given the burgeoning nationalism of the Axis powers; but in any case, impelled by world affairs and the public mood, the comic-book industry fashioned a number of patriotic heroes for popular consumption. These included Fighting Yank, descendent of a Revolutionary War soldier who received his powers from that long-dead ancestor; Captain America, a chemically enhanced human being created by the military as the first member of a proposed army of super-soldiers; and perhaps the most peculiar—and peculiarly American—hero of all, Uncle Sam, who first appeared in the aptly named *National Comics* in July 1940. Once these and other such characters were in place, it was a relatively simple matter to match them against Axis villains, anticipating the day when the United States surely would have to join the conflict in an official capacity. . . .

If rumors of war hinted at the end of escapism in American comic books, the fact of war presented empirical evidence of it. The questions at hand concerned national survival and the ability of the individual American to cope with the inevitable stress of awaiting an outcome. Comic-book heroes had new roles to play. Whereas crime fighting may have qualified as escapist fare during the 1930s (to the extent that crime was not a thing that touched every life), war was a different matter. Even the Depression had not affected the entire population, which may help to explain why popular culture could have afforded to ignore it. Moreover, crime had been the dilemma of local, state, and federal agencies, and the Depression had been widely viewed as a problem depending upon national political leadership for satisfactory resolution. In contrast, war concerned all Americans, and the cooperation of all would be required to insure a successful conclusion. It was not, as a rule, a time for cultural fun.

Comic Books' Contribution to the War Effort

Comic books brought much to the American cause. In addition to lending support to such necessary activities as bond drives and paper drives, comic books became an integral part of the Allied propaganda machine, emphasizing the need for a maximum war effort by portraying the enemy as the inhuman offspring of a vast and pernicious evil. Writers coined epithets like "ratzi" and "Japanazi," and artists drew rodentlike Japanese and bloated, sneering Germans. Japanese troops wore thick glasses and displayed prominent teeth, while German officers possessed monocles and dueling scars, much as they did in the wartime renditions of Hollywood filmmakers—although comic-book illustrators took greater liberties than Hollywood could, and to greater effect, given the nature of caricature. Comic books of the war years often bore dramatic covers—the full-color strangling of Hitler by a costumed hero, for example—which suggested an intensity of feeling but nevertheless frequently belied the contents of the issue. While the details of Hitler's agonized death might not (and probably would not) be recounted on the inside, comic-book heroes still could be relied upon to do something grand for the war effort and to wave the flag at regular intervals. Once the cover had stirred the blood, the slightest thing should serve well enough to keep it circulating, such books suggested.

Once America entered the war, the prevalence of heroes with superhuman powers created problems for comic-book publishers. Were the United States to unleash these impervious patriots upon the Axis, the war could reasonably be expected to end in an hour or less. Some explanation of why that would not happen had to be forthcoming if the credibility, and ultimately the utility, of the heroes were to be maintained, even among unsophisticated juvenile audiences. Publishers responded according to the characteristics of their heroes. Some risked having their less-powerful creations travel abroad, where protracted struggle could indicate that the enemy was altogether tougher than anyone had expected and explain why the war would not end quickly. Others allowed their heroes only indirect participation in the war, lest the plausibility of the characters be lost. On the one hand, Superman might indeed have asserted that "our boys" could handle the nasty business of war without his help; but on the other hand, it was also true that Superman's alter ego, Clark Kent, had managed to fail his preinduction physical, which had conveniently kept the "man of steel" from any involvement in a foreign theatre. While Superman did eliminate the occasional spy or saboteur at home, he did not routinely have the chance to strangle Hitler. Nor did Captain Marvel, who also stayed home and fought saboteurs, although in one story his creators did opt for allegory, allowing their hero to encounter a pair of malevolent trolls who closely resembled the leaders of Germany and Italy. They, it seemed, were ruining the lives of the rest of the trolls, who were ordinary, though small and subterranean, folk desiring only a return to peace in their time. And so forth and so on, in as many permutations and variations as there were costumed and powerful characters.

The War's Effect on the Comic Industry

War stimulated the comic-book industry, not only by providing much of the editorial matter but also by expanding the audience for comic books. Hundreds of thousands of comic books were shipped to American service personnel around the world. True, the books were inexpensive and portable and thus logical fare for troops in transit; but, as well, they satisfied the requirement which dictates that popular culture appeal to the lowest common denominator, in this case the individual with limited language skills and the capacity to respond to only a narrow range of cultural symbols. The mobilization of a total of some 16 million Americans by war's end suggested a number of possibilities to comic-book publishers, and they made every effort to capitalize on them. The quality of their product was of no concern in that economic environment.

Sending comic books to military personnel testified to the utility of the medium in raising morale through patriotic fervor, even if it should be achieved through appeals to racism. Laden as they were with unlikely heroic models, comic books could still inform about unity on the home front and indicate the extent to which American soldiers were glorified in a predominantly domestic medium. Even an illiterate could discern from comic books the virtue of the American cause and the sterling qualities of the American fighting man. Comic books served up a four-color version of a war in which the issues were black and white; they questioned nothing; and they dealt almost exclusively in happy—which is to say, victorious—endings. If this were indeed the "last good war," the comic books of the period bear witness to the accuracy of the label.

The war changed the appearance of comic books, probably because so many servicemen read them. By 1945, their artwork had developed a sexual orientation remarkable in a medium ostensibly still intended for juvenile audiences. A typical wartime cover might reveal in the foreground a scantily clad woman, tied with ropes or chains, at the mercy of some leering Axis villain, while in the background an American hero struggled forward, intent upon her rescue. The woman's clothing inevitably was torn to reveal ample cleavage and thigh, her muscular definition enhanced by forced contortion into some anatomically impossible position. Sometimes, her clothing was completely ripped away, leaving her to face her tormentor clad only in her unmentionables—which, presumably, gave added incentive to that struggling hero back there. The stories inside rarely if ever fulfilled the promises of such a cover, but they usually paid sufficient attention to female secondary sex characteristics to warrant a fellow's perusal.

The End of the Golden Age

World War II may have ended in 1945, but in comic books it raged on for another year or two, until publishers had exhausted their backlogs of war-related stories. But by then, they had created a serious problem for themselves. By 1946 or 1947 readers, whether they were children or belonged to the older audience built by the war, were jaded by the redundant deeds of redundant heroes. The costumed types, pale copies of Superman and Batman to begin with, had exhausted the dramatic possibilities of the medium as well as of their individual personae by having done, in four action-packed years, everything that anyone could imagine them doing. By the end of the war, comic-book heroes had been pushed to all manner of improbable pastimes, including tearing Axis tanks in half and leaping from one aircraft to another in the middle of a dogfight. Such foolishness continued for awhile, thanks to those backlogs, but it was simply too much for readers to bear, and comic-book sales plummeted.

Once the backlogs were exhausted, heroes had to return to crime fighting to make their contributions to society—and thus to earn their keep, for what good is a hero who does not practice his trade? But in the wake of a world war, that was nothing if not anti-climactic. Any number of heroes fell by the way, unable to pull their weight on an issue-to-issue basis. The survivors retained a loyal following, but a small one by comparison to what once had been. The very survival of comic books may well have been problematical in the minds of some publishers after 1945.

But of course the medium did survive, and it did so by adapting to a new socio-cultural climate with a radically different psychological construct. The war had brought current affairs into the comic pages, and there could scarcely be retreat from that, owing to the circumstances of war's end. Hiroshima and Nagasaki had rather emphatically illustrated the futility of the kind of escapist fantasy prevalent before 1940. Comic books, like other entertainment media, could not ignore what the world had become, nor could they effect a return to simpler times. Who needed a superman when we, with our atomic bombs, had become supermen? Comic-book publishers were willing to change, to adjust their focus, because they supposed that there was plenty of money still to be made. But first, they had to relearn their constituency. Like most other Americans, they had to discover what the nation had become, in consequence of victory.

3

The Beginning of the Cold War: The Red Menace and the Nuclear Threat

Hollywood and the Cold War

Joyce A. Evans

After World War II ended, relations between the United States and its former ally, the Soviet Union, plummeted, since the two nations represented the opposing ideologies of capitalism and communism. As the Cold War began, tension over the Soviets' development of nuclear weapons and concerns about possible communist infiltration swept America. In 1947 the government created the United States Information Agency, whose goal was to shape public opinion by popularizing anticommunist themes.

In 1947 the House Un-American Activities Committee (HUAC), concerned that Hollywood might become a source of communist propaganda, began investigating the movie industry for evidence of communist influence. Many politically liberal filmmakers and actors were blacklisted from work in the industry. In response, the major film studios released a series of anticommunist films, such as *The Red Menace* and *I Was a Communist for the FBI*. These films generally failed at the box office, perhaps indicating that Americans did not wholly embrace Cold War propaganda. However, the films helped restore Hollywood's patriotic image. And after the start of the Cold War, patriotism meant anticommunism.

Joyce A. Evans holds a Ph.D. in communication and teaches courses on popular culture, Hollywood film, and communication theory at the University of California at San Diego. The following selection is

■

from her 1998 book *Celluloid Mushroom Clouds: Holly-wood and the Atomic Bomb.*

THE COLD WAR AS THE GENERALIZED POLITICAL, social, and military fearfulness that resulted from the international rivalry between the United States and the Soviet Union developed an accompanying ideology that directly affected Hollywood studios and film content. Anticommunist themes and the fear of outside aggression and internal subversion became increasingly linked to issues of atomic technology and its capabilities. These issues formed the basis of a common dominant ideology, a constructed belief system, which was openly perpetuated by many social institutions as a "universal order" or "universal truth" that organized, explained, and reaffirmed the world, "making us understand the existing social order as well as imposing it upon us," [according to literary critic Roland Barthes].

A Fundamental Ideological Clash

A major ideological clash was inevitable when the United States and the Soviet Union emerged as the world's two major power centers after 1945. Although conflict is not the necessary result of a two-power scenario, the superpowers' commitments to ideologically opposed systems, with each nation advocating and actively working to export its own system, made confrontation impossible to avoid. Both superpowers were determined to [, as Charles Olson writes in *The Cold War . . . and After,*] "rearrange the pattern of political relationships in the world in accordance with what each conceived to be the absolute truth." This fundamental difference in point of view could not help but find expression in ideological conflict.

Both the United States and the Soviet Union concentrated on building "spheres of influence," usually via overt economic aid and often covert military aid. On the part of the United States, such aid was designed to contain the spread of Marxism, whereas the Soviets used their aid for exactly the opposite purpose, to spread the ideology of Marxism. Although this overt expansionism was a manifestation of the power struggle between the two nations, expansionist policies could not be sustained on either side without a supporting ideology. As Edward Thompson points out in *Beyond the Cold War*: "The confrontation of the superpowers has, from its origin, always had the highest ideological content: ideology . . . has motored the increment of weaponry, indicated a collision course. . . . In both camps, ideology performs a triple function: that of motivating war preparations, of legitimating the privileged status of the armorers, and of policing internal dissent."

The leading powers of each country were committed to an economic system that was the antithesis of the other. And in the name of ideology, each escalated the contest, justifying both expansionism and the arms race as the key to survival. The U.S. doctrine envisaged a world elaborately organized under law into a peaceful society of states, committed to free will, enterprise, and personal responsibility for one's actions. "Americanism" was conceptualized as idealistic, emotional, future-oriented, and optimistic; it glorified the dogma formulated by the Declaration of Independence and the Preamble to the Constitution. Convinced that the American way of life was superior to all others, it seemed logical and even philanthropic to export these beliefs and values to an anxious world.

On the other hand, communism's worldview was of a classless society where all lived and were treated as equals, with world order postulated as feasible and inevitable. The Soviet Union considered the ideal of communism as the basic motivation of all policy and was moved to action on behalf of its image of the truth. It was Marxist ideology, and the Soviet Union as its leading proponent, that posed a direct threat to the American way of life, which was based on private ownership and a free-enterprise system. Both of these national doctrines were universally applicable, leaving no room for the toleration of nonbelievers or for the compromise of their differences. The Cold War rapidly grew to become a way of life, an environmental factor to be factored into all conceptualizations of the contemporary world. The world was politically polarized, or at least was viewed by many as such.

The Arms Race

Much Cold War rhetoric and rationale pivots on the competition for superiority in weaponry. Gregg Herken writes that the Truman administration viewed the atom bomb as a means to practice atomic diplomacy, as a bargaining chip or as the ultimate weapon should diplomacy fail. Since many scientists and military specialists predicted a twenty-year monopoly on the technological and practical development of the atomic bomb, this diplomatic mandate was based upon the fact of American exclusivity concerning the bomb. Although this monopoly was destroyed in 1949 with the Soviet detonation of its own bomb, this "winning weapon" idea persisted into the postmonopoly period. The end of the monopoly caused no serious reappraisal of the central role of nuclear weapons in American foreign policy: The emphasis was merely shifted to a competition in the stockpiling of large quantities of more and more powerful weaponry. For example, for President Eisenhower, the "winning weapon" became the hydrogen bomb rather than the atom bomb. The hydrogen bomb was presented by the Eisenhower administration as a means to protect civilization, as a way to regain weapons superiority over the Soviet Union, and as a tool to further promote American initiatives in the Cold War.

In selling the American public on the idea of atomic weapons testing, specifically of testing within the United States, the government promoted Cold War sentiments. The buildup of nuclear weapons was accompanied by constant assurances to the American people that such a program was in the interests of democracy. First, the strong anticommunist sentiments developing within the culture were played up—the critical need for testing was emphasized for a strong national defense against potential Soviet aggression. Second, nonmilitary benefits and peaceful uses of nuclear technology were stressed by politicians and bureaucrats, who based their claims upon the already existing utopian ideals regarding nuclear technology. Finally, citizens were being constantly assured that all testing and nuclear development was conducted with the utmost concern for health and safety, with absolutely no potential risk of radioactive fallout.

Anticommunism played a major role in the justification of atomic testing and in convincing the public that nuclear development was necessary for security, even at the risk of fallout exposure. After the Soviets tested their bomb, named "Joe One," in the fall of 1949, the National Security Council (NSC) in Washington wanted a test site more militarily secure and closer to home than the Marshall Islands in the Pacific. When Nevada was chosen as a site, the AEC quickly stepped in to act as a public relations agency for atomic testing. In light of what was perceived as Soviet aggression in postwar international developments, many branches of government worked to foster a suspicious attitude toward the Soviets in their policies. Anticommunist activities by Congress included the actions of the HUAC and the investigations into individuals, programs, and agencies led by Senator Joseph McCarthy from 1950 to 1954. Known as "Tail Gunner Joe," McCarthy contributed to creating a climate propitious to the selling of the atomic bomb.

The Government and Anticommunism

Several laws were also enacted that reinforced Cold War paranoia and, consequently, atomic development and testing. In 1950, the McCarran International Security Act required members of the Communist Party to register with the Subversive Activities Control Board, by which they could be denied passports and employment in defense companies. By 1954, Congress had passed the Communist Control Act, making membership in the Communist Party a felony. Another factor that helped to foster a strong anticommunist sentiment was the government's preoccupation with issues of internal security. Such concern with security is exemplified by Executive Order 10450, issued by President Eisenhower in 1953, under which the mere suspicion of treachery brought termination of employment. Eisenhower later boasted that 2,200 "security risks" had been eliminated from government service. In this climate, Julius and Ethel Rosenberg were convicted and executed for passing Manhattan Project secrets to the Soviets during the war.

All major government organs utilized Cold War ideology in conveying the danger of the communist threat to the public. The military aided in the creation of the Cold War environment, for example, during the war games and maneuvers conducted at the Nevada atomic test site—the aggressor enemy was always portrayed as a communist force. Soldiers were indoctrinated from the beginning with the belief that should another major war appear, it would be fought against the communists. The AEC reminded the American people in press releases issued throughout the 1950s of the danger of letting down their defenses. For example, a statement issued in 1955 before the Congressional Committee on Atomic Energy reads: "Soviet Russia possesses atomic weapons; there is no alternative but to maintain our scientific and technological progress and keep our strength at peak level. The consequences of any other course would imperil our liberty, even our existence."

Public Opinion and Anticommunism

Widespread public animosity toward the Soviet Union developed after World War II, nourished by many politicians of both parties, by large segments of the mass media and the religious press, and by negative interpretations of Russian actions. In May 1946, 58 percent of Gallup's sample responded that "Russia is trying to build herself up to be the ruling power of the world" whereas only 29 percent chose the more favorable view that Russia is "just building up protection against being attacked in another war." By October 1947, the percentage choosing "ruling power" had risen to 76 percent and the percentage choosing "protection" had dropped to 18 percent. A Gallup poll reported in late 1948 an "almost unanimous belief that Russia is an aggressive, expansion-minded nation."

Because communism was presented as having world domination as its goal, proposals to improve relations with Russia were viewed with skepticism or hostility. The communists were seen as inherently untrustworthy: Conciliatory gestures on their part were camouflages to hide preparations for war. According to a 1949 Gallup poll, 60 percent of the sample believed that Russia did not want peace; by 1955, this had risen to 80 percent of the sample.

In the United States, government agencies such as the United States Information Agency (USIA) attempted to popularize anticommunist themes in an effort to shape public opinion domestically and abroad. The power of the word was seen as a potent influential force, and terms such as "freedom," "democracy," and "the free world" became the arsenal in the "war to win men's minds and souls." This belief in the persuasive strength of words and ideas demonstrates the heavy ideological basis of the Cold War. In an address to the USIA in 1953, President Eisenhower said that the American system would eventually win the Cold War because of its "greater appeal to the human soul, the

human heart, the human mind." The anticommunist propaganda campaign launched by the USIA in the early 1950s had
three primary objectives: to promote the American ideal, to
sketch out the adversary's characteristics, and to illustrate the
strategies, dangers, and consequences of communism.

Entertainment and the National Interest

Although the agency's operating assumptions concentrated on a
worldwide effort to "sell the United States to the world, just as
a sales manager sells a Buick or a Cadillac," the domestic media
were not excluded from its mission. All entertainment not in the
"national interest" was discouraged, with much criticism falling
on Hollywood's film output as propagating dramatic stereotypes
and unfavorable impressions of American life. The USIA stated
in a summation of its objectives: "If Hollywood film output is
harmful, the USIA should prevent harmful films from being
produced." However, the agency could not directly modify the
content of commercial films. Indeed, some of Hollywood's
products were even seen as advancing the USIA's objectives, the
agency being fully aware that audiences could learn values indirectly by watching films with no overt political content.

Special emphasis was placed upon the consequences of losing the Cold War, and the ultimate loss was conceived as being subjected to a nuclear sneak attack. At the same time, the
impression judiciously permitted to gain currency was that the
Cold War would some day culminate in a major crisis, perhaps
an all-out war against communism, out of which either the
United States would emerge victorious or the world would
come to an end in mutual nuclear obliteration. In this manner,
while the U.S. media indoctrinated the American public, it
also engendered an atmosphere of paranoia borne out of the
understanding that if the Cold War were lost and communism
were not contained, civilization "as we know it" would all but
cease to exist. Thus, the American public was browbeaten into
accepting the position of the government and its ability to
steer the country through the ideological perils that lay ahead.

Hollywood and HUAC

The performance of the Hollywood film industry at this time
can be viewed as that of a commercial enterprise responding to

political and economic pressure in the pursuit of larger profits. The industry had enjoyed prosperity after the war as attendance increased and studios prospered. Fears in Hollywood that peace would be a commercial disaster were not fulfilled, and 1946 turned out to be, in box-office terms, the most successful year in the history of the film industry. The annual profits announced by eight major film companies totaled over $125 million, which, when compared to the average annual figure of $35 million in the 1930s, was a tremendous increase.

However, in 1949 economic troubles began to develop, and the 1950s were devoted to attempts at economic recovery. Compounding the economic problems were the political purges initiated by the HUAC in 1947, resulting not only in studio blacklisting but also in the avoidance of controversial social topics. The blacklist reflected the nation's general insecurity, its image of the Soviet Union as an entity ready to devour the country and of communism as a constant and pernicious threat. Affected by the financial insecurity caused partly by the introduction of television, Hollywood's behavior can be seen as an attempt to pacify the government while the industry confronted its own economic problems.

The political climate of the 1950s was typified by the political purge initiated in 1947 by the HUAC; the stated purpose of the purge was to investigate communist propaganda in Hollywood films. Led by J. Parnell Thomas, the HUAC turned its attention completely to Hollywood in 1945 and 1946, citing the movie industry as one of the country's main centers of communist propaganda. The hearings featured fourteen friendly witnesses, whose purpose was to provide evidence that communism was running rampant in Hollywood and in Hollywood's films. Showcased in Washington before live microphones, the witnesses charged that pro-Soviet and communist propaganda had been deliberately promoted in various films produced during and after World War II. From each witness, the HUAC sought support to outlaw the Communist Party and to blacklist party members.

The Blacklist

Throughout the hearings, the committee attempted to get Hollywood leaders to approve of a blacklist, and in November

1947 the members of the Association of Motion Pictures issued a statement claiming that they would eliminate all subversives and communists from their industry. Public opinion seemed to favor anticommunist measures, and Louis B. Mayer stated that the fear of film censorship and the belief that public opinion could be appeased led to the blacklisting of studio personnel suspected of communist sympathies. The American Legion quickened the industry's decision to blacklist by threatening a national boycott of films and pickets in front of theaters.

Besides the Hollywood Ten, the ten screenwriters who were purged for refusing to cooperate with the committee, members of the Committee for the First Amendment as well as 208 actors of the Actors' Division of the Progressive Citizens of America, who had taken out an advertisement in *Daily Variety* to protest the hearings, were threatened. In 1951 and 1952, new names were continually added to the blacklist. Studios also compiled a "graylist," which contained the names of noncommunists who had radical leanings. These individuals weren't fired outright but were moved to innocuous positions and barred from promotion; many had great difficulties in finding new jobs.

The HUAC's emphasis gradually shifted to claims that communists had been feeding on the reputations and the financial assets of various Hollywood individuals. In the past, funds had been raised by Hollywood employees to aid refugees from fascist countries or to buy ambulances for Spanish loyalists. This aid was perceived by members of the HUAC to have benefited the American Communist Party. The content of the movies became of far less importance to the HUAC than the naming of names. Many of the hearings were televised, which helped spread and popularize the suspicion that communists were indeed working within the Hollywood industry. These hearings continued sporadically until 1954, and by the time they were over 90 prominent industry figures had testified and 324 alleged communists had been blacklisted by the studios. During this time, the HUAC's hold on public opinion had been considerably strengthened by a series of national and international events: the fall of China to the communists, the first successful atomic explosion by the Soviet Union, the outbreak of the Korean War, and the conviction of Alger Hiss. The combined force of these events helped the committee achieve its goal of eradicating liberalism and radicalism in Hollywood.

The Studios' Response

The studios were terrified that the charges of communism would wreck their industry. The American Legion and other right-wing groups promised to picket any movie if the name of any suspected communist appeared in the screen credits, and outside investment in any movies that could conceivably be a target for pickets would be nonexistent. Hollywood producers feared that millions of potential moviegoers would shun the films that the American Legion condemned. The legion, with three million members, rallied support in communities all over the country, conducting a letter-writing campaign and informing sponsors about the political affiliations of many entertainers. Demonstrations outside theaters showing Charlie Chaplin's *Monsieur Verdoux* resulted in the movie being withdrawn from circulation. Many theater owners and television stations were even dissuaded by the legion from showing Chaplin's silent films. After the 1951 hearings, the heads of the five major studios promised not to hire anyone who had taken the Fifth Amendment and asked the legion for its own files of suspects so that the "loyalty" of employees could be checked against the legion's files.

To a certain extent, Hollywood's motives in complying with the HUAC can be seen as an attempt to fend off political interference while the industry attacked a more significant problem—that of declining attendance. In 1949, a decline began as movie attendance fell to 70 million per week from 90 million per week the year before. The decline hit bottom in 1958 at 39.6 million moviegoers per week and stabilized at 40 million in the 1960s.

The reasons for this decline are numerous. Television was a major factor. A 1951 survey concluded that theaters dropped 1 percent of their gross income for each 2 percent of homes within their market that had acquired a television. Personal disposable income was also being diverted from movies to other items such as radios, televisions, and automobiles. During the period from 1929 to 1945, expenditures for motion picture admissions accounted for an average of 21.2 percent of the typical family's recreation budget, while home entertainment expenditures, covering the purchase and repair of records, musical instruments, and radios was 12.7 percent. Just after World War II, there were limits on goods available, and movies were an ever present alternative; for this reason, audiences were not terribly selective about the pictures they saw. However, by 1949, home entertainment and motion picture admissions had reversed their relative standings; home entertainment expenditures now accounted for 24.3 percent of recreation expenses whereas motion picture admissions accounted for only 12.1 percent.

Since the Hollywood industry was confronted with both political and economic pressure, it sought to pacify the political sector while trying to adjust to new economic realities. Perhaps the studios felt that they could not afford to irritate political authorities at a time when public opinion seemed to favor anticommunist measures. In any event, films with even moderately liberal trappings were no longer produced, since the HUAC investigations had implied that patriotic producers should avoid films with controversial social content. Even a conservative producer like John Ford was uneasy because, almost ten years earlier, he had directed *The Grapes of Wrath* (1940), which could be interpreted as a leftist film and which had been attacked when it was released. *Variety* sarcastically described the situation: "Hollywood's brass has been so busy trying to prove that the picture industry is a right-living, right-thinking and right-producing community that they have gone far out of their way to offend no one—whether it be Thomas, the Catholic Church, the Jews, the Negroes, the President, the American Dental Society, or the Institute of Journeymen Plumbers of America."

The Anticommunist Films

Before the HUAC hearings, Hollywood had shown an interest in films that explored social problems such as anti-Semitism, racism, and demagoguery, and many such films, including *Gentlemen's Agreement* (1947), *Crossfire* (1947), *All the King's Men* (1949), and *Home of the Brave* (1949) had been box-office hits. After the hearings, it has been speculated that producers lost their courage, and as a result the percentage of socially relevant films declined. Instead, "pure entertainment" films were emphasized, and a series of anticommunist pictures were quickly produced to repair the movie industry's tarnished image. According to John Cogley, the number of movies focusing on social issues decreased drastically between 1947 and 1954, although more than fifty anticommunist films were produced during those same years.

These anticommunist films utilized themes such as atomic development and security; they include *The Red Menace* (1949), *I Was a Communist for the FBI* (1951), *The Whip Hand* (1951), and *My Son John* (1952). Such films capitalized on the stereotypes of communism developed in part by the USIA. American communists were portrayed as dark, unkempt, irrational fanatics aggressively intent upon destroying the United States. The public showed little interest in the Cold War fare, but as a public relations gimmick, the pictures helped restore Hollywood's image among the industry's right-wing guardians.

Americans' Views of Nuclear War

Toni A. Perrine

Just as Americans have alternately embraced and rejected war in general, so too have their views on nuclear weapons shifted since the atomic bomb was first developed in the 1940s. After the United States dropped two atomic bombs on the Japanese cities of Hiroshima and Nagasaki in 1945 in order to end World War II, Americans initially held the new weapons in awe. In the 1950s this soon gave way to fear of the effects of radioactive fallout and worry that the Soviet Union might attack the United States with nuclear weapons. By the late 1950s and early 1960s, several major antinuclear films and novels had become popular. By the late 1960s, however, antiwar protestors had turned their attention from nuclear weapons to the escalating conflict in Vietnam.

In 1979 an accident at the Three Mile Island nuclear power plant near Harrisburg, Pennsylvania, coupled with rising tensions between the United States and the Soviet Union, led to a renewed anxiety over nuclear energy and nuclear weapons. In the early 1980s several films with post-apocalyptic settings were produced, and even video games and music videos incorporated images such as mushroom clouds. With the collapse of the Soviet Union in 1991, cultural awareness of nuclear issues once again subsided, demonstrating Americans' remarkable willingness to ignore their nation's enormous nuclear capabilities.

Toni A. Perrine is a professor in the department of

■

film and video production at Grand Valley State University in Allendale, Michigan. The following essay is excerpted from her book *Film and the Nuclear Age: Representing Cultural Anxiety.*

GENERAL ATTITUDES TOWARDS THE POSSIBILITY of nuclear disaster are cyclical and largely correspond to political events. The immediate post-Hiroshima/Nagasaki period was one of jubilation at the surrender of Japan, attributed to the use of atomic bombs, and awe directed toward the power of the new weapon. Later, paranoia and fear of the still unknown destructive capability of atomic weapons developed. Americans began to worry about the morality of using a weapon of such destructive power against civilian populations as well as the possibility that such a weapon might be used against them. The late forties were marked by a numbing of nuclear awareness marked by acceptance of the bomb as a condition of existence which was supported by the fact that the United States still held a monopoly on nuclear weapons. When the Soviet Union successfully tested its first atomic bomb in 1949, the initial phase of the nuclear arms race developed in the context of the extreme anti-communist sentiment of the early Cold War. Development of the hydrogen bomb by the U.S. in 1950 was considered necessary to stay ahead of the Soviet Union in the nuclear arms race (although research on the "superbomb" began before it was known that the Soviets had succeeded in their efforts). According to [cultural historian] H. Bruce Franklin, "Since the atomic 'secret' allegedly had been stolen for the Russians by Communists like the Rosenbergs, anyone against nuclear weapons in America must be at best a Communist dupe."

A Growing Sense of Alarm

In the early 1950s, atmospheric testing of nuclear weapons in Nevada and Utah was contaminating towns and ranches downwind of the test sites and the danger of fallout gradually became known to the public. A fear of radioactive fallout was exacerbated by the Bravo test of March 1, 1954 which spread lethal levels of fallout over a 7,000 square mile area of the Pacific and caused radiation sickness in Japanese fishermen aboard the *Lucky Dragon*. Fallout from nuclear weapons testing became a domestic controversy and led to a national movement against such testing, as well as the growth of national organizations like SANE, the National Committee for a Sane Nuclear Policy. Many films from the period, for example, *Them!* (1954), depict mutant creatures spawned by radioactivity who threaten human civilization.

Despite the fear associated with the Soviet development of the atomic bomb, nuclear arms strategists acknowledged that the Soviets did not possess a delivery system capable of attacking the United States with nuclear weapons. The mid 1950s were marked by a diminished attention to the threat posed by nuclear weapons based, in part, on the fact that only conventional warfare was carried out by the U.S. in Korea, despite widely articulated support for use of the atomic bomb to end the "police action" quickly. Another reassuring factor was Eisenhower's "Atoms for Peace" initiative, which included a large-scale public relations program intended to demonstrate the "sunny side of the atom," that is, how nuclear power could

Science Fiction and the Cold War

The Cold War, basically an extension of the Second World War, . . . helped to create a climate that generated interest in science fiction. The rivalry between the USA and Russia in rocket development brought home to the public the reality of space-age technology, particularly when newsreel shots showed a fast-receding earth photographed by automatic cameras from missiles fired from the White Sands testing site, and, later, white rats and monkeys floating in space. The Cold War also produced an atmosphere of anxiety and paranoia: anxiety mainly caused by the ever-present possibility of atomic war between the two superpowers and the resulting global destruction; paranoia caused by the fear of communist subversion, an invasion from within by people who looked like ordinary Americans

be used in beneficial ways, particularly to provide cheap and limitless energy for American consumers.

The year 1957 marked yet another phase in nuclear awareness engendered by the fear that accompanied the development of Soviet satellite technology. According to [historian] Spencer Weart,

> There was no single moment when everyone began to feel they were living on the edge of universal death . . . for many [Americans] the turning point came in October 1957 when the first Soviet Sputnik orbited overhead. Unstoppable missiles had seemed like something for a remote science fiction future; suddenly they seemed like something that could drop on the United States next year. The American press erupted in an almost hysterical alarm.

Beginning in the late 1950s, American culture was once again pervaded by nuclear themes as evidenced by the appearance of films like *On The Beach* (1959), *Fail Safe* (1964) and *Dr. Strangelove: Or How I Learned to Stop Worrying and Love the Bomb* (1964) and novels like Helen Clarkson's *The Last Day*

but who were actually the pawns of an alien power. . . .

As a result of these fears most of these sf films of the 1950s reflect a number of basic themes: the atomic bomb and its after-effects; the effects of atomic radiation; alien invasion and possession by aliens; and world destruction. . . .

After the first few years, during which all the major sf cinema themes were established—alien invasion in *The Thing, War of the Worlds, It Came from Outer Space*; alien possession in *Invaders from Mars, Invasion of the Body Snatchers*, and *I Married a Monster from Outer Space*; the effects of atomic radiation in *The Beast from 20,000 Fathoms, Them!*; world destruction in *When Worlds Collide*; and a bit of everything in *The Day the Earth Stood Still*—the film genre endlessly repeated itself with cheaper and less impressive variations on the same themes.

John Brosnan, *Future Tense*, 1978.

(1959) and Walter Miller's *A Canticle for Leibowitz* (1959). In 1961, President Kennedy initiated a massive civil defense program. A profusion of yellow and black fallout shelter signs were visual reminders of the omnipresent danger of nuclear war as well as the officially sanctioned belief that large segments of the population could survive nuclear war with the proper preparations. This period ended abruptly around 1964. The Cuban missile crisis in 1962 had resulted in the United States and Soviet Union "backing down" from the brink of the nuclear abyss. According to Franklin, "The outcome of the Cuban missile crisis amounted to a tacit bilateral arms-control agreement . . . out of this crisis emerged a quest for coexistence and detente." In addition, the 1963 Limited Test Ban Treaty sent nuclear testing underground and out of the public eye. The emphasis on civil defense which had characterized the fifties and early sixties was quietly dropped from the national agenda in the face of mounting evidence that to "duck and cover," or even to build bomb shelters and stock fallout shelters, were inadequate measures against the destructive potential of nuclear weapons. The fear of possible nuclear war and actual radioactive fallout that had been building since the mid-fifties suddenly dissipated in the absence of the constant reminders that had typified the preceding decade.

A Period of Apathy

The period from 1964 to the mid-seventies saw a sharp decline in cultural expressions of nuclear awareness. Historian Paul Boyer suggests "the prevailing American stance toward the nuclear war threat from 1963 to well into the 1970s was one of apathy and neglect" and cites several reasons for the diminished, almost nonexistent, cultural concern with the possibility of nuclear destruction during this period. Underground testing resulted in the illusion of diminished risk and a loss of immediacy. The nuclear arms race was theoretical, remote, largely invisible and was therefore ill-suited to the insatiable visual demands of television. The promise of a world transformed by atomic energy was the other side of the psychological balancing act largely perpetrated by the Nuclear Regulatory Commission and adjunct government agencies. Other factors included the paradoxical comfort of the deterrence theory and the fact that the

Vietnam War demanded all of the energy of potential antinu-clear activists and in fact, preoccupied the nation at large. The 1967 Outer Space Treaty (banning all space based weapons) and the 1968 Nonproliferation Treaty (restricting nuclear weapons technology to those nations which already belonged to the "nu-clear club") further defused nuclear fear.

Other efforts towards bilateral arms control continued through the seventies and culminated in the two Strategic Arms Limitations Treaties (SALT I signed in 1972 and SALT II in 1979). Franklin summarizes this process as follows:

> The Strategic Arms Limitations talks ground on year after year until both sides accepted the fact that neither could achieve military superiority, agreed that they were at parity, and defined parity precisely in types and numbers of weapons.

Journalist Robert Scheer credits the arms control process in the era of detente with the decreased cultural preoccupation with nuclear war. During this period, according to Scheer,

> Most Americans found it relatively easy to avoid thinking about nuclear annihilation. There was comfort in the knowledge that somewhere in the midst of all the inter-minable SALT talks, our respective leaders were trying to cut whatever deal was possible in the interest of their, and our, survival.

This is not to suggest that the actual nuclear threat dimin-ished during this period, in fact, it continued and grew in terms of the destructive capability of both superpowers, but only that outward manifestations of public concern were few or nonexistent. Nor can we conclude [, writes Boyer,] that "nuclear fear ceased to be a significant cultural force in these years. [Psychiatrist and author] Robert Jay Lifton may well be right in his speculation that the denial of nuclear awareness . . . affects a culture as profoundly as acknowledging it does."

The Renewed Antinuclear Movement

The above set of circumstances began to break up in the late 1970s. The year 1979 witnessed the Three Mile Island acci-dent and the unsettling though coincidental release of the film *The China Syndrome* depicting just such an accident a few weeks later. The withdrawal of SALT II from the Senate after the Soviet invasion of Afghanistan also occurred in 1979 and set up a major roadblock to disarmament talks. Vietnam was largely resolved as a national political issue. A vigorous anti-nuclear weapons movement was developing in Western Europe which renewed Americans' awareness to the danger and implicated them as purveyors of nuclear arms in nations where the people did not want them. Three Mile Island also initiated a growing awareness of the interconnection between nuclear power and nuclear weapons. The election of Ronald Reagan in 1980 is frequently cited as another primary factor in the increased nuclear anxiety that characterized the early eighties. The Reagan administration's bellicose rhetoric, including talk of limited nuclear war and the deployment of tactical nuclear weapons in Western Europe, did little to minimize nuclear fears. Reagan's announcements of the Strategic Arms Reductions Talks (START), which called for a total restructuring of Soviet forces along lines favorable to existing American forces in May of 1982, and the Strategic Defense Initiative (SDI or "Star Wars"), a space-based nuclear weapons defense system in March of 1983, destabilized detente and renewed public attention to the possibility of nuclear war.

In the 1980s, this dramatic shift in political consciousness once again found widespread cultural expression. Many people again struggled towards [, as Boyer puts it,] "unlocking the closed door of nuclear memory." A number of films in the early eighties, *The Road Warrior* (1982), *Aftermath* (1982), *The Day After* (1983), *Survival Zone* (1983), *Testament* (1983), and *Warriors of the Wasteland* (1983) to name a few, explicitly make reference to the idea of nuclear war. A veritable explosion of books on nuclear issues were published during this period. Nuclear awareness and activism most recently peaked in this country around 1983. The nuclear freeze movement gained strength amid vigorous public discussion about nuclear issues. This phase of the cycle waned with the major upheaval in geopolitical relations related to the break-up of the Soviet Union in the early nineties.

After a sustained and serious effort to confront our nuclear predicament, nuclear fear and its most potent symbol, the mushroom cloud, were more likely to be put to the service of music videos and arcade games than progressive narrative films. According to Franklin, "In the 1980s, the most popular fictions about nuclear war are survivalist fantasies, mixing virulent anti-communism, sadistic pornography, and propaganda for Star Wars" which he suggests "actually seem to celebrate nuclear holocaust." Boyer concludes that the major difference between the eighties and the late forties was that

> The holocaust scenarios of the 1980s, by contrast, are only too plausible. Indeed, our stabs at imagining possible nuclear futures are continually outdistanced by actual developments. In the 1940s, imagination raced ahead of reality; in the 1980s, reality races ahead of imagination.

The End of the Cold War

For many people, the end of the Cold War signaled the end of the possibility of nuclear war in the context of a "new world order" in which the United States clearly emerged as the dominant military power. The Persian Gulf War of 1991, in which the use of tactical nuclear weapons was never ruled out, confirmed a widely supported American commitment to militarism and high tech weaponry. Predictably, cultural manifestations of nuclear fear also declined in the 1990s. Despite periodic headlines about "deviant" states like Iraq and North Korea attempting to produce nuclear weapons, nuclear testing by France, or the possibility that "loose nukes" could fall into the hands of unscrupulous nations or terrorist groups, a general awareness of the nuclear threat has been quiescent in the 1990s. The 1995 controversy that erupted over the proposed Smithsonian exhibit of the *Enola Gay* [the plane that dropped the first atomic bombs on Japan] to commemorate the fiftieth anniversary of the bombings of Hiroshima and Nagasaki was short-lived. This latest retreat from confronting our nuclear capability is consistent with American cultural and historical patterns of denial, disavowal and fear.

4

EXAMINING *POP* CULTURE

The Vietnam War: U.S. Ambivalence Is Reflected in Popular Culture

An Overview of Vietnam Films

Rob Edelman

The war in Vietnam was America's longest, most controversial war and only military defeat. As such, Americans have held a variety of opinions toward the war which have shifted over the years. Films about Vietnam have often been controversial but can provide valuable insight into Americans' changing views of the conflict.

The first movies set in Vietnam, most of which were filmed in the 1950s, are similar to World War II films in their portrayal of the U.S. military, albeit with the addition of anticommunist overtones. A few years after the war's end, however, most Americans viewed the war as a mistake, and this was reflected in the popular entertainment of the late 1970s. In films of the era, such as *The Deer Hunter* and *Apocalypse Now*, the war is portrayed as horrible and pointless, while Vietnam veterans are stereotyped as emotionally troubled or even sociopathic. By the late 1980s, several films, such as *Platoon* and *Full Metal Jacket*, attempted to give a deeper portrayal of the Vietnam experience, with mixed results. Perhaps the most important role of Vietnam films is to remind Americans of the mistakes that were made regarding the war, so that they will not be repeated.

Film critic Rob Edelman has written for a variety of newspapers and magazines and is a contributing editor to *Leonard Maltin's Movie and Video Guide*. The following is excerpted from one of Edelman's essays in *The Political Companion to American Film*.

■

Excerpted from "Vietnam War Films," by Rob Edelman, in *The Political Companion to American Film*, edited by Gary Crowdus (Chicago: Lake View Press, 1994). Copyright © 1994 by Gary Crowdus. Reprinted by permission of the publisher.

BLUE THUNDER (1983), AN ACTION-ADVENTURE thriller, features Roy Scheider as a Los Angeles police helicopter pilot. Scheider's character happens to be an ex-GI who had fought a decade or so earlier in the rice paddies of Vietnam. He is, as the reviewer in *Variety* so pointedly noted, "a Vietnam vet who, for once, is portrayed as a hero." Now that the Vietnam War no longer remains the lead story on each evening's news, films about Vietnam and its aftermath do serve one valuable purpose: they are a means by which the American public may be reminded that 57,000 of the nation's youth died in a war they really had no business fighting. Beyond this, however, and relating more specifically to the content of each film, the depiction by commercial filmmakers of Vietnam-era soldiers, or of the American scene back when the president was Lyndon Johnson or Richard Nixon, has for the most part been simplified and distorted. While the essential nature of practically all Vietnam War films not made by John Wayne or before the Tet Offensive is that of hopelessness, with distressingly rare exception Hollywood's portrayal of Vietnam has been, like the war itself, sorely misguided.

The most celebrated Vietnam films to date include Michael Cimino's *The Deer Hunter* (1978), Hal Ashby's *Coming Home* (1978), Francis Coppola's *Apocalypse Now* (1979), Oliver Stone's *Platoon* (1986) and *Born on the Fourth of July* (1989), and Stanley Kubrick's *Full Metal Jacket* (1987). These are neither the first nor the only features that attempt to explore America's longest, most controversial war and only military defeat. Hollywood had employed Vietnam as a backdrop for standard action fare as early as two decades before most Americans had ever heard of Ho Chi Minh. . . .

Box Office Poison

The two most representative films of the era are Samuel Fuller's *China Gate* (1957) and Joseph L. Mankiewicz's *The Quiet American* (1958), both products of the McCarthyite Fifties. *China Gate* is an action drama in which foreign legionnaires blow up a communist ammunition dump. It is a fascinating curio, the depiction of a Vietnam torn between godless communism and a wonderful Christian tradition in which peasants thrive materially and spiritually. (Rather than featuring Asian performers in the leads, Angie Dickinson plays "Lucky Legs," a Eurasian saloonkeeper, while Lee Van Cleef is Major Chan, a communist "war lord.") *The Quiet American* is a bastardization of Graham Greene's fine novel. In the original, an idealistic young American contributes "economic aid" to Vietnam via terrorist bombings. But in the film he's a private citizen, not a United States government employee, an innocent framed by the communists.

Then, in the mid-Sixties, came Lyndon Johnson's escalation of the war. While Hollywood celebrated the exploits of American GIs in dozens of features released during World War II and, to a lesser extent, Korea, Vietnam remained virtually absent from American movie screens. After all, Americans would not pay to see movies about a war that was brought into their living rooms every evening by Walter Cronkite. Sadly, at its height, only one Hollywood feature even dared to deal with Vietnam: *The Green Berets* (1968), a vapid, laughably absurd melodrama of saints (the righteous Americans, led by John Wayne) versus sinners (the dastardly commie VC [Vietcong]). In its essence, *The Green Berets* is just a formula Western set in Asia rather than Wyoming or Arizona, with Aldo Ray's Green Beret Sergeant Muldoon replacing Victor McLaglen's U.S. Cavalry Sergeants Mulcahy in *Fort Apache* (1948) and Quincannon in *She Wore a Yellow Ribbon* (1949) and *Rio Grande* (1950).

Three years after the signing of the Paris Peace Accords, America's escapade in Vietnam still remained taboo in Hollywood. Feature films directly addressing Vietnam were considered box office poison because the wounds of the war were still too raw. The nation had to pause, and decompress, before accepting cinematic explorations of its meaning. Then, in the late Seventies, came a spate of Vietnam-related films, most of which depicted the war as a nightmare, a mismanaged, half-hearted effort rife with demoralized, stoned-out soldiers and corrupt, pig-headed commanders.

Placing Blame

By this time, the war had come to be regarded as a mistake even in conservative circles. America had, after all, lost. Blame had to be placed. *The Boys in Company C* (1978), for example, is crammed with finger pointing. In the film, soldiers die while transporting a top-priority convoy of beef and Jim Beam whiskey for a general's birthday party, and level an "enemy" village inhabited by women and children. Officers are more concerned with body counts than with actually winning the war, and one even arrogantly sputters to a subordinate, "These people die at my command." Their South Vietnamese counterparts conspire to smuggle heroin to the United States in the body bags used for corpses. Nevertheless, there is no real depth here, no real exploration of the who, what, and why of Vietnam. The two most famous late-Seventies features actually set in Vietnam are *Apocalypse Now* and *The Deer Hunter*. Despite their artistic merit, and their Cannes Golden Palms and Academy Awards, both are laden with stereotypes and inaccuracies. The former is more a reworking of Joseph Conrad's *Heart of Darkness*, with technically incorrect battle scenes and undisciplined GIs. Robert Duvall's Colonel Kilgore is a cartoon caricature: a warmonger with a Civil War hat, bugle, and surfboard; while the various soldiers are off in their stoned-out worlds. The visuals may be sumptuous, but the core of the film is empty and artificial.

The Deer Hunter, the epic saga of three Ukrainian-American steelworkers and their experiences in Southeast Asia, does attempt to define the meaning of nationalism and honor. The result, however, is far too ambiguous. The finale, which sums up the tenor of the film, is exasperatingly unclear. In it, the remaining characters sing "God Bless America." Are they doing so halfheartedly—they have, after all, just buried one of their own—or are they reaffirming their faith in their country? Additionally, the Vietcong are portrayed as comic strip villains, one-dimensional sadists and goons.

Vietnam Vet Films

While Vietnam veterans have not been as absent from the screen as GIs in combat, their lot also was stereotyped to the point of absurdity. The celluloid warriors of the World War II era, in which America was united behind an inarguably just cause, returned home winners and liberators. They came back to their families and communities, readjusted to life in civvies, and went on to happy-ever-after futures. Any vet with problems had to be physically disabled: blind John Garfield in *Pride of the Marines* (1944); handless Harold Russell in *The Best Years of Our Lives* (1946); paralyzed Marlon Brando in *The Men* (1950). Each spurns his girl out of apprehension, yet she stands by him in hopeful finales. . . .

Vietnam veterans on celluloid have never been so idealized. From such exploitation fare as 1971's *Chrome and Hot Leather* ("Don't Muck Around With a Green Beret's Mama! He'll take his chopper and ram it down your throat!"), *The Visitors* (1972), *Welcome Home, Soldier Boys* (1972), *The Zebra Force* (1977), and *The Exterminator* (1980) to the three *Rambo* films (released in 1982, 1985 and 1988) and *The Big Chill* (1983), Vietnam vets have been characterized, at worst, as killing machines, crazed Charles Manson clones, motorcycle-riding rapists and thugs or, at best, as aimless, impotent drug dealers or suicidal depressives. Typical is the vet protagonist in *The Stunt Man* (1980), a fugitive from justice described by David Denby as "a seedy Vietnam veteran with fear in his eyes." "You wanna get home for Thanksgiving," he says, "you better figure the guy comin' at ya is gonna kill ya. Learned that from the gooks." He also notes, "I don't know nothin' about Germans. Where I was, we only raped gooks."

In *Rolling Thunder* (1977), William Devane stars as an emotionally deadened ex-POW who returns home after wasting away for eight years in a prison camp. He finds an America as violent as the country he has just left: he sees his wife and son senselessly murdered by thieves and, with his former cellmate, sniffs out the killers. The film concludes with a lengthy bloodbath in a Mexican brothel. One plot device in *Rolling Thunder* serves to symbolize a particularly odious celluloid myth: even the Vietnam vets who are heroes remain powder kegs, itching to explode. This vet's hand is at one point mashed by a mechanical waste-disposal unit, and he in a perverse way seems to thrive on the pain. After all, his years in the prison camp have whetted his appetite for this sort of thing. His mangled hand is replaced by a hook, which he sharpens into a very lethal weapon. . . .

During the Sixties, when Vietnam was still winnable, a great and honorable American adventure, cinematic villains often were depicted as hypocritical hippie types who had somehow managed to shirk military service. It was a time when wearing long hair was in itself a political statement, and anyone embracing the counterculture was automatically suspect. The movies reflected this perception. In *Coogan's Bluff* (1968), the heavies are pot-smoking, acid-tripping "love children" who really would love to inflict violence on sheriff Clint Eastwood. But less than a decade later the war was lost, and moviemakers were not concerned with the reasons why. Someone had to be blamed, and veterans (rather than State Department policy-makers or military strategists) were the most convenient scapegoats. In *The Enforcer* (1976), the third Dirty Harry film, Eastwood tangles with the Peoples' Revolutionary Strike Force, a Symbionese Liberation Army clone whose leader, as he tersely notes, "was in Vietnam, likes combat." . . .

Vietnam Documentaries

Overall . . . an understanding of the folly of Vietnam has been best depicted on celluloid via documentary. As a record of life on the front line, Pierre Schoendorffer's *The Anderson Platoon* (1967) is a superior chronicle of soldiers fighting, living, and dying. From a point of view of issues, politics, and morality, or the experiences of those who actually served in Vietnam, the real truths of the war are most successfully explored in Emile de Antonio's *In the Year of the Pig* (1969), Michael Rubbo's *The Sad Song of Yellow Skin* (1970), Joseph Strick's *Interviews with My Lai Veterans* (1971), Peter Davis's *Hearts and Minds* (1974), Glenn Silber and Barry Alexander Brown's *The War at Home* (1981), and Bill Couturie's *Dear America* (1988).

These films movingly and successfully reveal the political or experiential reality of Vietnam. *The War at Home*, for example, is a brilliantly edited, year-by-year collage of the growing antiwar movement in Madison, Wisconsin. It features such images as a 1964 LBJ for president television spot promising to keep the peace—on October 21st of that year, the President declared, "We are not about to send boys nine or ten thousand miles away from home to do what Asian boys ought to be doing for themselves"—followed by Americans arriving and fighting in the rice paddies to the accompaniment of Barry Sadler's Top 40 hit "Ballad of the Green Berets."

If documentarians were concerned with exploring the truths of Vietnam, Hollywood filmmakers were soon to be portraying the war in an appalling, revisionist manner. It was back to Cowboys and Indians in *Uncommon Valor* (1983), with Gene Hackman whipping some vets into shape to sneak into Laos and successfully rescue American POWs. The Asians fall like Apaches attacking the cavalry in a John Wayne Western and America can now be proud, can regain its honor, can actually, incredibly, "win" the war. Similar scenarios followed in *Missing in Action* (1984), starring Chuck Norris, and *Rambo: First Blood Part II*. And, in *Rambo III*, John Rambo even finds a new war. This one may be set in Afghanistan, but it's against the same, tired old enemy: one-dimensional commie swine who claim they "try to be civilized" as they smack their prisoners of war senseless.

Platoon and *Full Metal Jacket*

Perhaps inspired by the phenomenal popularity of Rambo—*Rambo: First Blood Part II* opened in a record-breaking 2,074 first-run moviehouses in May 1985, which was, ironically, the tenth anniversary of the fall of Saigon—the movie industry's movers and shakers thought it good business to produce a number of big-budget features set in Southeast Asia. The key titles from this period are *Platoon* and *Full Metal Jacket*. As in *The Boys in Company C*, each attempts to define the war by vividly establishing a time and place. Each is a brutally realistic war drama, crammed with sights, sounds, and details. From a dramatic perspective, *Platoon* and *Full Metal Jacket* are startlingly effective, and stunningly acted. From a political perspective, however, neither offers a point of view beyond the concerns and motivations of its characters.

Platoon is the story of Chris (Charlie Sheen), an eighteen-year-old college dropout who arrives in Vietnam. His platoon is divided into two camps: those who follow Sergeant Barnes (Tom Berenger), a psychotic, morally degenerate killing machine, and those who follow Sergeant Elias (Willem Dafoe), a combat veteran who nevertheless has managed to maintain a sense of compassion and humanity. Chris is initiated into the ways of war; eventually, Barnes murders Elias, and Chris becomes determined to put a halt to Barnes's tyranny.

Full Metal Jacket is the story of a group of Marines who have volunteered for Vietnam combat. The film's first lengthy section depicts their boot-camp training, presented as a dictatorship run by the maniacal, foul-mouthed drill instructor (Lee Ermy, who appears in a not dissimilar role in *The Boys in Company C*). He praises two ex-Marines who became noted murderers—mass-murderer Charles Whitman, and alleged presidential assassin Lee Harvey Oswald—and whips his charges into a unit of dehumanized killers. Once in Vietnam, the men—including the film's most sensible character, played by Matthew Modine—exhibit a complete lack of humanity, an appalling disregard for human life. . . .

The various individuals in all these scenarios undergo horrific experiences. As such, each film might be labelled as "anti-war." Yet their creators fail to either offer an overview of the war or place their characters within a global framework. In so doing, they ignore the questions that are the keys to their characters' experiences. What about this particular war? How did America come to be involved in Vietnam? War might be hell, but is American involvement in this specific war worth the hell that these characters endure? . . .

More Realistic Portrayals of Vietnam Vets

During the late Eighties, a number of films did attempt to deal with Vietnam veterans more honestly and compassionately. *Born on the Fourth of July* [has as] its hero . . . a real person: Ron Kovic, who was paralyzed while in combat, and who is transformed from idealistic flag-waver to eloquent antiwar spokesperson. *In Country* (1989) may feature a shell-shocked, reclusive vet (Bruce Willis), but he is sympathetically rendered; additionally, the scenario focuses on the attempts of his niece (Emily Lloyd), whose father was killed in Vietnam, to understand the war. *Jacknife* (1989) chronicles the plight of a pair of veterans who served together in the war, and what happens when one begins to date the other's sister. These vets may all have "problems," but they deviate from the well-worn veteran-as-psycho cliché, and this is rare and refreshing. . . .

At the same time, all of these films do focus on veterans who are alienated from the mainstream. We still rarely in films see characters whose status as Vietnam vet is of little or no consequence to their roles in the story. And given the nature of Vietnam, perhaps we never will.

Films like . . . *Jacknife*, *In Country*, and *Born on the Fourth of July* also serve as sobering reminders of what the legacy of the war against Saddam Hussein might be if American military strategy had been as inept as it was in Vietnam. One would imagine that many a Vietnam vet—particularly those who were bloodied by the war psychologically, if not physically— must have felt a special pain upon hearing George Bush, in the exaltation of victory, proclaim that America can now "put Vietnam behind us."

Gardens of Stone (1987) is the sole mid-to-late-Eighties Vietnam film not focusing on Vietnam veterans that comments on the grander scheme of the war. James Caan plays a troubled career Army sergeant, a combat veteran who . . . loves the service but despises the war. Symbolically, his current job is to oversee the men assigned to an elite corps that presides over Arlington Cemetery's Tomb of the Unknown Soldier, and escorts the coffins of Vietnam's fallen to their final resting places.

The Importance of Remembering Vietnam

For anyone who lived through the Vietnam War, *Gardens of Stone, Hearts and Minds*, and even *The Deer Hunter* and *The Boys in Company C* will revive long-buried memories and feelings. They will be uncomfortable, even painful: Chicago in 1968, perhaps, or Kent State, or Nixon watching quarterbacks and cheerleaders while thousands pleaded for peace at his White House doorstep, or the war coming alive, day after day, year after year, on TV's evening news.

An occasional stirring of these memories and feelings is necessary, even healthy, because the Vietnam experience must never become a few paragraphs buried in history books. On one level, of course, the war must be laid to rest. The president of the United States is no longer named Johnson or Nixon, and a whole new set of national priorities exist. Still, as with the Holocaust, it remains imperative that young Americans, who might assume that the Tet Offensive is the latest strategy of the Los Angeles Rams, learn about Vietnam so that the same mistakes of purpose and policy will not be repeated. For this reason alone, we must never allow ourselves to "Put Vietnam behind us."

Vietnam Protest Songs of the 1960s and 1970s

H. Ben Auslander

By the late 1960s, rising casualty figures and draft quotas for the war in Vietnam fueled a growing anti-war sentiment among young Americans. Popular folk musicians gave voice to this counterculture by performing anti-Vietnam songs and other general protest music that emerged as rock and roll became a venue of social criticism. The first protest song to mention Vietnam by name debuted in 1964, and the number of Vietnam protest songs peaked in 1967. That year, CBS tried to ban folksinger Pete Seeger from performing his antiwar allegory "Waist Deep in the Big Muddy," but relented after accusations of censorship. The anti-Vietnam song genre died out after 1970 as Americans became increasingly weary of the war and exasperated by the failed efforts to end it.

   H. Ben Auslander was studying American literature at the University of Delaware when he published the *Journal of American Culture* article from which this selection is excerpted.

ROCK MUSIC CAME OF AGE IN THE SIXTIES. OUT-growing its childhood of simple four chord progressions and inane lyrics, rock evolved into a complex art form that affected the lives of millions, simultaneously reflecting and shaping their political and social attitudes. Much has been written about

■

Excerpted from "If Ya Wanna End War and Stuff, You Gotta Sing Loud: A Survey of Vietnam-Related Protest Music," by H. Ben Auslander, *Journal of American Culture*, Summer 1981. Reprinted by permission of Popular Press.

the maturing of rock, but one area that has curiously been ig-
nored is the study of protest music of the sixties, especially that
directed against the war in Vietnam. A possible explanation of
this neglect may lie in the difficulty of sorting Vietnamese-
related material from general social protest music, the two genres being so inextricably intertwined. If one accepts as one's research criterion examining only those songs directly related to
Vietnam, many important songs may be overlooked. On the
other hand, to include all protest music of the period would be
to obscure the significance of songs directly related to the war.
A middle approach, then, one including material directly concerning the American involvement in Vietnam and also those
songs depicting the side-effects of that involvement, would
seem to be the best means of assessing the genre.

The First Vietnam Protest Songs

The roots of anti-Vietnam protest music can be traced back to
those folksingers involved in the Civil Rights and nuclear disarmament movements of the late fifties and early sixties. Faced
with the often violent reactions to civil rights demonstrations
and the continual threat of thermonuclear annihilation by the
Soviet Union, folk artists such as Bob Dylan, Joan Baez, Phil
Ochs, Malvina Reynolds, Peter Yarrow, Paul Stookey and
Mary Travers alike took firm stands for racial brotherhood and
international peace. It was neither difficult nor unexpected,
then, for such artists to shift the emphasis of their messages
from "Stop oppressing our black brothers," to "Stop oppressing our yellow brothers," and from "Ban the bomb," to "Stop
the war in which we'll probably use the bomb," as the American involvement in Southeast Asia intensified.

Phil Ochs' "Talkin' Vietnam Blues" had the distinction of
being the first protest song to directly refer to Vietnam by
name. The release date of that song is of particular note—
April 1964, a full four months before the Gulf of Tonkin incident and the first major escalation of the American presence in
Vietnam. Whether Ochs was mystically prescient or simply an
excellent socio-political prognosticator is irrelevant; one
should note, however, that rather than reflecting or attempting
to direct public opinion, Ochs consistently seemed to second-
guess it throughout his career.

Ochs' second album, released in February 1965, included two songs directed against the Selective Service that were both to become classics of the Draft Resistance movement: "The Draft Dodger Rag" and the album's title song, "I Ain't Marchin' Anymore." As draft quotas rose throughout the year, Ochs' outspoken anti-draft attitudes came to be shared by more and more potential draftees.

1965 was also the year of one of the decade's most controversial Top Forty hits, "Eve of Destruction." Released less than a month after the triumph of Gemini 4, the song included lyrics such as, "You may leave here for four days in space/But when you return it's the same old place." The singer-songwriter, Barry McGuire (another folksinger, formerly lead vocalist for the New Christie Minstrels), and his songs were immediately lambasted by the news media for expressing

"We Gotta Get Out of This Place"

During the course of the Vietnam War, many rock and roll songs that were hits back in the United States proved popular among American troops as well, but for dramatically different reasons. Whereas a song's popularity in the States was often based on its melody, the personality of the artist, and other factors that had little to do with lyrical content (although that could be a factor as well), certain songs became popular at American bases in Vietnam precisely because their lyrics seemed to encapsulate certain basic impressions about the nature of the war and the feelings of its participants. One of the most popular of these songs was undoubtedly The Animals' "We Gotta Get Out of This Place," a work that became an anthem of sorts among American troops. . . .

Although the . . . song was certainly popular in the United States (it reached number 13 on the *Billboard* singles charts), its impact was far greater in Vietnam. Years after its release, the song remained a staple in Saigon jukeboxes and fire base tape players. Indeed, the lyrics of the

excessive pessimism, and the song was subsequently denied airplay on many radio stations. While attracting far less attention, "The War Drags on," by the English folksinger Donovan was also released during 1965, an event significant in that it marked the first time American listeners were exposed to criticism of the war from a non-American artist.

The Antiwar Movement in Full Swing

By 1966 America's involvement in Vietnam was no longer a peripheral issue for rock music's listeners. Rising troop commitments, rising casualty figures, and rising draft quotas all contributed to the growing anti-war sentiment of the young. The youthful "counterculture" became increasingly disaffected with and alienated from the "establishment" of American culture, and that schismatic tension was forcefully represented in

song—which spoke longingly of the unnamed narrator's thirst for an alternative to his present situation—neatly and simply encapsulated much of the despair and desperation felt by American servicemen in Vietnam, and its raucous sound lent sing-a-longs a cathartic quality absent from more sedately paced songs.

Both during and after the war some observers from both military and civilian backgrounds have speculated that such songs had a corrosive impact. Les Cleveland [the author of *Dark Laughter: War in Song and Popular Culture*], for instance, commented that "as a source of oppositional ideology, songs like the Animals' 'We Gotta Get Out of This Place' may have contributed to the demoralization of some of the troops in Vietnam." Others, though, contended that the disillusionment stemmed from more tangible aspects of the American soldier's environment, and that the popularity of "We Gotta Get Out of This Place" and other songs of its ilk was simply a reflection of the hopes, fears, and experiences of those soldiers.

Kevin Hillstrom and Laurie Collier Hillstrom, *The Vietnam Experience: A Concise Encyclopedia of American Literature, Songs, and Films*, 1998.

several of the year's songs. Once again Phil Ochs expressed the feelings of many with his satiric songs "I'm Going to Say It Now" and "Love Me, I'm a Liberal," while the Fugs (charter members of rock and roll's lunatic fringe) pushed humor to the limit with their song "Kill for Peace." In sharp contrast to the Fugs' technique of aesthetic overkill, Simon and Garfunkel released two quiet anti-war songs, "Seven O'clock News/Silent Night" (juxtaposing the well-known Christmas carol with the narration of a topical and depressing news broadcast) and "Scarborough Fair/Canticle" (whose anti-war message was so subtly presented that many never realized they were listening to a protest song). As troop commitments and troop ceiling figures increased, so did rock's attention to the war.

In terms of both the number of songs recorded and the artistic expressiveness of those songs, 1967 was decidedly the peak year for Vietnam-related protest music, and in the autumn of that year, public attention was concentrated on protest songs and singers like never before. The public's attention was first focused on the genre when CBS television executives banned folksinger Pete Seeger from performing his anti-war allegory, "Waist Deep in the Big Muddy," on a September *Smothers Brothers Comedy Hour* broadcast. The executives held to their position that the song's reference to the "big fool" (i.e. Lyndon Johnson) was disrespectful and should not be broadcast on a prime time show, then finally caved in under charges of censorship and allowed Seeger's performance.

During that same September Joan Baez's latest album, *Joan*, was receiving a good deal of attention, in part for the song "Saigon Bride." As if to counter charges that protest music was nothing more than noisy rock and roll, Baez co-wrote and recorded this gently poetic ballad about an American soldier bidding farewell to his Vietnamese wife as he leaves to fight in the jungles. Arlo Guthrie, son of the famous folksinger Woody Guthrie, also came into the public spotlight that month with the release of his first album, *Alice's Restaurant*, including the enormously popular monologue, "The Alice's Restaurant Massacre." Guthrie's humorous burlesque of the judicial system, the Selective Service, and the military establishment won him instant acceptance with the anti-war movement, but neither that movement nor the singer himself was spared a few stinging remarks (best expressed, perhaps, in a remark to his audience after an unsuccessful attempt at an audience sing-along—"If ya wanna end war and stuff, you gotta sing loud"). The month's activity was capped by the release of Peter, Paul and Mary's "The Great Mandala (The Wheel of Life)," a hagiographic account of a draft resister's life and death. Two months later, Country Joe and the Fish's song, "The I-Feel-Like-I'm-Fixin'-To-Die Rag," was released, providing the late sixties' anti-war demonstrators with an unofficial marching song.

The Decline of Protest Music

Until 1968 the growth and popularity of protest music closely paralleled escalation of American involvement in Vietnam, then unexpectedly its intensity began to wane while the war's continued to increase. The number of anti-war songs recorded declined and those that were released lacked the immediacy and forcefulness of their predecessors. One explanation may be that performers and audiences alike were physically and spiritually exhausted by the war against the war and simply did not want to be reminded of the conflict any more than was necessary. Another possible reason may be that many shared the sense of manic resignation expressed by Phil Ochs in his last anti-Vietnam song, "The War is Over."

Whatever the cause, protest music declined as the sixties ended and the seventies began. Apart from Joni Mitchell's "The Fiddle and the Drum", 1969 was an aesthetically lean year for protest music. By the time of the Kent State University murders by National Guardsmen in May 1970, the anti-Vietnam song genre was effectively dead. The last Vietnam-related protest song, Neil Young's "Ohio" (recorded by Crosby, Stills, Nash, and Young and released as a single during the summer of 1970), commemorated the four murder victims and simultaneously provided an epitaph for the entire anti-Vietnam peace movement.

The First "Living Room War": Vietnam on Television

Daniel C. Hallin

Television was still in its infancy during the Korean conflict; not until the Vietnam War did the major networks get a chance to cover another war. Daniel C. Hallin, the author of *The "Uncensored War": The Media and Vietnam*, describes the controversy over what effect TV coverage of the war had on public opinion toward Vietnam. The conventional wisdom is that TV brought home the "horror of war" and thus turned people against the war effort, but Hallin notes that graphic portrayals of violence or suffering were rare in TV coverage of Vietnam. He also describes television series of the 1980s that dealt with the war.

VIETNAM WAS THE FIRST "TELEVISION WAR." THE medium was in its infancy during the Korean conflict, its audience and technology still too limited to play a major role. The first "living-room war," as Michael Arlen called it, began in mid-1965, when Lyndon Johnson dispatched large numbers of U.S. combat troops, beginning what is still surely the biggest story television news has ever covered. The Saigon bureau was for years the third largest the networks maintained, after New York and Washington, with five camera crews on duty most of the time.

■

Reprinted from Daniel C. Hallin, "Vietnam on Television," in *The Encyclopedia of Television*, edited by Horace Newcomb, published by Fitzroy Dearborn, by permission of the publisher.

What was the effect of television on the development and outcome of the war? The conventional wisdom has generally been that for better or for worse it was an anti-war influence. It brought the "horror of war" night after night into people's living rooms and eventually inspired revulsion and exhaustion. The argument has often been made that any war reported in an unrestricted way by television would eventually lose public support. Researchers, however, have quite consistently told another story.

Images of Violence and Suffering

There were, to be sure, occasions when television did deliver images of violence and suffering. In August 1965, after a series of high-level discussions which illustrate the unprecedented character of the story, CBS aired a report by Morley Safer which showed Marines lighting the thatched roofs of the village of Cam Ne with Zippo lighters, and included critical commentary on the treatment of the villagers. This story could never have passed the censorship of World War II or Korea, and it generated an angry reaction from Lyndon Johnson. In 1968, during the Tet Offensive, viewers of NBC news saw Col. Nguyen Ngoc Loan blow out the brains of his captive in a Saigon street. And in 1972, during the North Vietnamese spring offensive, the audience witnessed the aftermath of an errant napalm strike, in which South Vietnamese planes mistook their own fleeing civilians for North Vietnamese troops.

These incidents were dramatic, but far from typical of Vietnam coverage. Blood and gore were rarely shown. Just under a quarter of film reports from Vietnam showed images of the dead or wounded, most of these fleeting and not particularly graphic. Network concerns about audience sensibilities combined with the inaccessibility of much of the worst suffering to keep a good deal of the "horror of war" off the screen. The violence in news reports often involved little more than puffs of smoke in the distance, as aircraft bombed the unseen enemy. Only during the 1968 Tet and 1972 spring offensives, when the war came into urban areas, did its suffering and destruction appear with any regularity on TV.

For the first few years of the "living room war" most of the coverage was upbeat. It typically began with a battlefield roundup, written from wire reports based on the daily press briefing in Saigon—the "Five O'Clock Follies," as journalists called it—read by the anchor and illustrated with a battle map. These reports had a World War II feel to them—journalists no less than generals are prone to "fighting the last war"—with fronts and "big victories" and a strong sense of progress and energy.

The battlefield roundup would normally be followed by a policy story from Washington, and then a film report from the field—typically about five days old, since film had to be flown to the United States for processing. As with most television news, the emphasis was on the visual and above all the personal: "American boys in action" was the story, and reports emphasized their bravery and their skill in handling the technology of war. A number of reports directly countered Morley Safer's Cam Ne story, showing the burning of huts, which was a routine part of many search-and-destroy operations, but em-

The First Television War

Vietnam, the first rock 'n' roll war, was also the first television war, with combat footage on the nightly news. Johnson tried assiduously to manage television coverage of the war, pundits debated endlessly about whether television had "brought the war home" or had trivialized it as just another interruption in the stream of commercials, and whether the scenes of carnage and the reports of American atrocities had numbed its audience or had increased anti-war sentiment or street violence. Television reporting was brutally attracted to scenes of violence and dissent—they made good pictures. By the end of the 1960s political groups denied conventional access to the media had recognized the staged act of violence as an effective means of gaining attention. Terrorism happened for the television camera.

Richard Maltby, ed., *Passing Parade*, 1989.

phasizing that it was necessary, because these were Communist villages. On Thursdays, the weekly casualty figures released in Saigon would be reported, appearing next to the flags of the combatants, and of course always showing a good "score" for the Americans.

"Bang-Bang" Coverage

Television crews quickly learned that what New York wanted was "bang-bang" footage, and this, along with the emphasis on the American soldier, meant that coverage of Vietnamese politics and of the Vietnamese generally was quite limited. The search for action footage also meant it was a dangerous assignment: nine network personnel died in Indochina, and many more were wounded.

Later in the war, after Tet and the beginning of American troop withdrawals in 1969, television coverage began to change. The focus was still on "American boys," to be sure, and the troops were still presented in a sympathetic light. But journalists grew skeptical of claims of progress, and the course of the war was presented more as an eternal recurrence than a string of decisive victories. There was more emphasis on the human costs of the war, though generally without graphic visuals. On Thanksgiving Day 1970, for example, Ed Rabel of CBS reported on the death of one soldier killed by a mine, interviewing his buddies, who told their feelings about his death and about a war they considered senseless. An important part of the dynamic of the change in TV news was that the "up close and personal style" of television began to cut the other way: in the early years, when morale was strong, television reflected the upbeat tone of the troops. But as withdrawals continued and morale declined, the tone of field reporting changed. This shift was paralleled by developments on the "home front." Here, divisions over the war received increasing air time, and the anti-war movement, which had been vilified as Communist-inspired in the early years, was more often accepted as a legitimate political movement.

Walter Cronkite

Some accounts of television's role regarding this war assign a key role to a special broadcast by Walter Cronkite wrapping up his reporting on the Tet Offensive. On 27 February 1968, Cronkite closed "Report from Vietnam: Who, What, When, Where, Why?" by expressing his view that the war was unwinnable, and that the United States would have to find a way out. Some of Lyndon Johnson's aides have recalled that the president watched the broadcast and declared that he knew at that moment he would have to change course. A month later Johnson declined to run for reelection and announced that he was seeking a way out of the war; David Halberstam has written that "it was the first time in American history a war had been declared over by an anchorman."

Cronkite's change of views certainly dramatized the collapse of consensus on the war. But it did not create that collapse, and there were enough strong factors pushing toward a change in policy that it is hard to know how much impact Cronkite had. By the fall of 1967, polls were already showing a majority of Americans expressing the opinion that it had been a "mistake" to get involved in Vietnam; and by the time of Cronkite's broadcast, two successive secretaries of defense had concluded that the war could not be won at reasonable cost. Indeed, with the major changes in television's portrayal of the war still to come, television was probably more a follower than a leader in the nation's change of course in Vietnam.

Vietnam in Television Fiction

Vietnam has not been a favorite subject for television fiction, unlike World War II, which was the subject of shows ranging from action-adventure series like *Combat* to sitcoms like *Hogan's Heroes*. During the war itself it was virtually never touched in television fiction—except, of course, in disguised form on *M*A*S*H*. After Hollywood scored commercially with *The Deer Hunter* (1978), a number of scripts were commissioned, and NBC put one pilot, *6:00 Follies*, on the air. All fell victim to bad previews and ratings, and to political bickering and discomfort in the networks and studios. Todd Gitlin quotes one network executive as saying, "I don't think people want to hear about Vietnam. I think it was destined for failure simply because I don't think it's a funny war." World War II, of course, wasn't any funnier. The real difference is probably that Vietnam could not plausibly be portrayed either as heroic or as consensual, and commercially successful television fiction needs both heroes and a sense of "family" among the major characters.

An important change did take place in 1980, just as shows set in Vietnam were being rejected. *Magnum, P.I.* premiered that year, beginning a trend toward portrayals of Vietnam veterans as central characters in television fiction. Before 1980 vets normally appeared in minor roles, often portrayed as unstable and socially marginal. With *Magnum, P.I.* and later *The A-Team, Riptide, Airwolf* and others, the veteran emerged as a hero, and in this sense the war experience, stripped of the contentious backdrop of the war itself, became suitable for television. These characters drew their strength from their Vietnam experience, including a preserved war-time camaraderie which enabled them to act as a team. They also tended to stand apart from dominant social institutions, reflecting the loss of confidence in these institutions produced by Vietnam, without requiring extensive discussion of the politics of the war.

Not until *Tour of Duty* in 1987 and *China Beach* in 1988 did series set in Vietnam find a place on the schedule. Both were moderate ratings successes; they stand as the only major Vietnam series to date. The most distinguished, *China Beach*, often showed war from a perspective rarely seen in post–World War II popular culture: that of the women whose job it was to patch up shattered bodies and souls. It also included plenty of the more traditional elements of male war stories, and over the years it drifted away from the war, in the direction of the traditional concern of melodrama with personal relationships. But it does represent a significant Vietnam-inspired change in television's representation of war.

MASH: The Korean War as a Setting for Vietnam Satire

Rick Worland

The TV series *MASH*, a sitcom set during the Korean War, debuted on television just as the war in Vietnam was winding down. Running from 1972 to 1983, *MASH* became one of the most popular shows in the history of television, and this success was due in part to its ability to harness the antiwar mood of the nation in the wake of Vietnam. The show centered around a clearly pacifist theme, that of a group of doctors trying to save lives in the middle of a war. High-ranking officers on *MASH* were portrayed as inept and callous, while the show's most likable characters were pacifists of lower military rank who reveled in ridiculing anticommunist paranoia. Though ostensibly a comedy series, many episodes dealt with more serious themes such as the tension between patriotism and respect for human life.

Rick Worland is a professor of cinema at Southern Methodist University. His research has concentrated on film and television in the Cold War period.

IN 1968, DR. H. RICHARD HORNBERGER, WHO HAD worked as a surgeon in a mobile army surgical hospital during the Korean War, wrote a comic novel called *M.A.S.H.*, loosely

■

Excerpted from Rick Worland, "The Other Living Room Combat War: Prime Time Combat Series, 1962–1975," *Journal of Film and Video*, Fall 1998. Reprinted with permission. Endnotes in the original have been omitted in this reprint.

based on his wartime experiences. Seventeen publishers rejected the manuscript, and it was punched up by a ghost writer before publication under the name Richard Hooker.

Following the success of the Robert Altman/Ring Lardner, Jr., film version of *MASH* (1970), an irreverent, antimilitary comedy set in a Korean War field hospital, yet replete with allusions to Vietnam, Twentieth Century-Fox commissioned a television version supervised by veteran comedy writer Larry Gelbart and producer Gene Reynolds. The series debuted in September 1972. Despite poor ratings its first year, *MASH* slipped into an enviable hammock the next season between *All in the Family* and *The Mary Tyler Moore Show* and built Nielsen success thereafter, becoming a genuine television phenomenon that continued until its producers voluntarily retired the series in 1983. The two-and-a-half-hour series finale, aired on February 28, garnered an incredible 77 audience share, becoming the highest-rated program to that date.

MASH's Pacifist Overtones

MASH marked a significant departure from military sitcoms of the past. Rather than depicting the wacky exploits of putative fighting men, as in *Hogan's Heroes* or *McHale's Navy*, the series focused on a group of doctors and nurses led by Alan Alda's pacifistic Dr. Hawkeye Pierce. Here the troops numbered among their ranks a gentle priest, a bashful file clerk, and a pseudo-transvestite hoping to wangle a section-eight discharge. The series lampooned gung-ho warriors in the characters of the insipid Major Frank Burns (Larry Linville) and the grimly masochistic intelligence officer, Colonel Flagg (Edward Winter). Perhaps the show's single most telling evocation of the postwar mood came in "Officer of the Day" (24 September 1974), in which Hawkeye is charged with distributing the unit's monthly payroll yet repeatedly refuses to wear a pistol, as army regulations require.

Jamie Farr's Cpl. Max Klinger, who spent the first several seasons in dresses and heels, can be seen as a figuration of the draft resister, an individual who refuses incorporation into the military group, the fundamental ideological mission of traditional combat films. Like the Vietnam "short-timer," Klinger sees no greater purpose beyond staying alive until discharged.

His resistance, however, is founded on egoism—the military stifles his personal freedom—not moral or political opposition to the war. Still, Klinger's constant attempts to quit the army regardless of the duration of the war or its consequences and the ambiguous connotations of gayness make the character a wholly new figure in popular representations of war, both radical and disturbing for many despite the comic distance. . . .

Unlike earlier military comedies, *MASH* dealt overtly with the physical and psychological costs of war as the doctors treated countless young soldiers mangled in combat, while operating only a few miles from the front lines. To cope, the doctors used gallows humor, sometimes mere silliness, to retain their humanity and mental health. In "Dear Dad" (17 December 1972), Hawkeye writes home, "If jokes seem sacrilegious in an operating room, I promise you they are a necessary defense against what we get down here at this end of the draft board." In "The Interview" (24 February 1976), shot in black and white to simulate a 1950s newscast, the characters give a TV reporter their opinions about the war and their work—thoughts that juxtapose their hatred of the former with their pride in the latter and the absurdity of this condition. . . .

Fundamentally, a series that portrays doctors treating an unending stream of American casualties in a stalemated war spells defeat and failure. "O.R." (8 October 1974), produced without a laugh track, took place entirely in the operating room during an interminable shift. Deluged with wounded, the doctors saved some patients, lost others. In one memorable scene, Col. Henry Blake (McLean Stevenson) and Hawkeye decide to let a hopelessly injured soldier die rather than waste precious time and scarce plasma that could save several other men. Still, the motto of the 4077th, "Best Care, Anywhere," suggests Americans struggling pragmatically through arduous circumstances and emerging with honor and pride intact. *MASH* functioned so successfully on just this thematic tension. . . .

MASH and the Military Sitcom

Although uniforms were prevalent in TV entertainment in the '60s, military sitcoms outnumbered combat dramas. In 1965, the peak year of the form, eight different military comedies were running on the networks. Thereafter, although individual shows continued, the total number declined until the 1971–1972 season—after Kent State, Cambodia, the trial of Lt. Calley, and so on—when there were no programs, comic or dramatic, with servicemen as principal characters. The openly antiwar *MASH* appeared the next season.

Military sitcoms, from *You'll Never Get Rich* (CBS, 1955–1959) to *MASH*, revolved around a group of misfits, an unorthodox unit and its leader who laugh at traditional military discipline, flaunting regulations in a kind of childish fashion through activities usually involving drinking, gambling, and womanizing. Like Phil Silvers's Sgt. Bilko, Sgt. O'Rourke and Cpl. Agarn of *F-Troop* (ABC, 1965–1967) are money-hungry operators, eager for a fast buck. The troopers are the secret owners of the only saloon in Fort Courage and marketers of fake "Indian souvenirs" manufactured by their partners, the otherwise inept Hekowi Indians. In *McHale's Navy* (ABC, 1962–1966), the exploits of a PT boat crew in the South Pacific, the sailors lived on an island apart from the main naval base, the better to throw luaus with pretty nurses and to hide their houseboy, a genial Japanese POW. McHale's hedonistic gobs in their Hawaiian shirts, cocktails in hand, anticipate the identical leisure-time images of Hawkeye and friends on *MASH*.

In the traditional service comedies, criticism of the military wasn't directed at the institution itself but at inept individuals— the foolish Capt. Parmenter (Ken Berry) of *F-Troop*, the fuming, self-serving Capt. Binghampton (Joe Flynn) on *McHale's Navy*—creating a rather traditional populist lampoon of authority in the abstract. Rather than sensibly devoting their energy to fighting the enemy, the petty martinets try to force the rebel group to heel to strict military discipline and usually fail, not realizing that it is their very unconventionality that makes the mavericks great warriors or, in *MASH*, great doctors.

Then, too, criticism of the military was further reduced by the presence of a dignified higher authority, a wise general or admiral who recognized the results the heroes obtained and intervened when their witless commanders would punish harmless nonconformity. Significantly, the comic regiments actually fight on occasion—*F-Troop*'s cavalrymen sometimes stand off the ferocious "Shug" tribe, while McHale's crew destroys Japanese planes and ships. The combination of the proven if unorthodox warriors and the enlightened higher-ups left the institution essentially respected. The Capt. Bing-hamptons of the world will always be with us, amusing and annoying in equal measure, but no real reflection on the military as a whole.

MASH inverted these ideological structures. The inept commander, especially McLean Stevenson's Col. Henry Blake, became part of the misfit group, a respected surgeon and fellow nonconformist given to wearing a fishing hat adorned with lures, an icon of informality and relaxation. To call Henry Blake "unfit for command" became a compliment that gung-ho Majors Frank Burns and Margaret Houlihan's (Loretta Swit) insistence on the old meaning of the phrase could not change. More important, on *MASH*, higher authority was anything but wise and benign. Generals were venal, aloof, and unqualified. General Hammond (Herb Voland), seen in the early years of the show, was a hypocrite who was more interested in posturing for the press and lusting after "Hot Lips" Houlihan than in overseeing the welfare of the medical units.

In "Some 38th Parallels" (20 January 1976), an apt summation of the show's attitude toward top brass, Hawkeye takes revenge on a callous general who incurred needless casualties by dropping a helicopter-load of garbage on him. By contrast, in earlier service comedies, it was the middle-ranking Captain Binghampton figure who was regularly humiliated.

"That Old Crazy Asian War"

In "Sometimes You Hear the Bullet" (28 January 1973), Hawkeye is reunited with his boyhood pal Tommy Gillis, a war correspondent who is planning to write a book called "You Never Hear the Bullet," taken from a soldier's dying words. Meanwhile, into the operating room comes fresh-faced Pvt. Wendell Peterson (Ron Howard), a marine, as Hawkeye learns, who is actually too young to be in the service. The surgeon reluctantly agrees to keep the boy's secret until Tommy comes in badly wounded. When his friend dies, Hawkeye goes to the MPs and has Wendell sent home. "I'll never forgive you for this—not for the rest of my life!" says Wendell angrily. "Let's hope it's a long and healthy hate," Hawkeye replies.

"Sometimes You Hear the Bullet" marked an important breakthrough for the series, which prior to this episode, aired midway through the first season, was a more traditional service comedy with little of the drama and antiwar attitudes that would become its hallmark. Wendell is a gung-ho warrior eager to return to his outfit and "kill me some more gooks." "Wendell, another word for gooks is people," Hawkeye counsels. No one is allowed to spout such opinions unchallenged on *MASH*, yet, reflecting something twisted in American society, meanwhile, Andy Griffith's TV son, Opie, hungered for genocide.

MASH reflects a breakdown in the Cold War consensus in the aftermath of Vietnam. In the early years especially, anyone who speaks seriously of the officially stated goals of the war—repelling international communist aggression—is treated as deluded and dangerous. The more rabid one's anticommunist rhetoric, the louder the chuckles on the laugh track. This signified a substantial change in popular conceptions of the Cold War that should not easily be dismissed. Frank Burns was the usual fount of such pronouncements, whose irrationality and irrelevance were underscored by the fatuous character himself. [Professor of psychology and religious studies] Peter Homans says of Frank, "It is no surprise that he is a poor surgeon, a failure linked in some unspoken way to his adulation of militarism." In an operating-room scene punctuated by the roar of artillery, Frank gloats, "I hope we're really giving it to them, those little yellow Reds"; his fogged confusion of the meaning of "yellow" says much here. As the Wendell Peterson incident also indicates, enthusiastic Cold Warriors were apt to be perniciously tainted with racism.

MASH frequently ridiculed the Cold War intelligence/security establishment along the lines of hippie comedian George Carlin's much-stolen quip that "military intelligence is a contradiction in terms." The chief target was CID [Criminal Investigation Division] agent Colonel Flagg, who made several guest appearances. In "A Smattering of Intelligence" (24 March 1974), Flagg repeatedly injures himself deliberately, first to "infiltrate" the hospital, then to furnish an excuse to stay until his mission is completed. (Upon hearing Flagg once crashed a jeep into a brick wall and set himself on fire to investigate a hospital, Hawkeye marvels, "Is this person available for children's parties?")

And what brings Flagg to the 4077th—a vital assignment to thwart the latest communist conspiracy? No, he's come to shadow the agent of a rival American secret service man who is shadowing *him* because "they always try to pull a show-boat at appropriations time."

In "Yankee Doodle Doctor" (22 October 1972), an army photographic unit comes to the 4077th to shoot a documentary on the inspirational work of the medical staff. Frank Burns exults in an opportunity to supply grandiose narration for what emerges as a hollow propaganda piece. In retaliation, Hawkeye and company film their own version—an anarchic Marx Brothers farce with Hawkeye as Groucho, Trapper John as Harpo, and Frank's laudatory voice-overs juxtaposed with absurd images. In the end, however, Hawkeye is shown directly addressing the camera, insisting they are not "saints in surgical garb," just average men and women trying to do a good job and save lives. The story exudes cynicism with the mass media as much as with the military. In the wake of Vietnam, we easily assume the official version of events is apt to be shallow, misleading, and false.

Disdain for the media was a leitmotif of Robert Altman's *MASH*, presented through the device of loudspeaker announcements constantly blaring official nonsense, or invoking western imperialist messages while saccharine American pop tunes were sung in Asian tongues. Higher authority seemed at once ubiquitous and baffled, relying on an unceasing media barrage to retain its diminishing credibility and control. This device ("May I have your attention please?") was used in the early TV episodes but more clearly suggested that the skeptical soldier dutifully reading government-approved news and ludicrous military directives was no longer taken in by their nonsense.

At the coda of "O.R.," after the medical staff has been nearly overwhelmed with wounded soldiers, the loudspeaker broadcasts a summary of the war's changing command structure: "General Clark is relieving General Ridgway, who relieved General MacArthur." As Hawkeye and Trapper collapse in their bunks, the announcer adds editorially, "No one is relieving us, at all."

"The Operation Was Successful But . . ."

MASH remained a Nielsen powerhouse for more than a decade despite significant evolutions in characters and major cast changes. These adjustments were not without impact, however. The most telling change was the replacement of Henry Blake with Col. Sherman Potter (Harry Morgan). Blake's death in the plane carrying him home to his family ("Abyssinia, Henry," [18 March 1975]) was the high-water mark of *MASH*'s antiwar thematic. The decision to kill Henry at the moment of his apparent delivery employed an old yet always effective device of the war drama but was bold for a sit-com in a system that preferred good cheer and happy endings in everything from commercials to the nightly news. Ironically, the Henry Blake character—befuddled yet decent and professionally accomplished, an ideal American type who could have been played by the young Jimmy Stewart—died in the spring of 1975, about six weeks before Saigon fell to the North Vietnamese army.

Markedly older and wiser, Sherman Potter, Regular Army, former cavalryman, installed a benevolent yet firm patriarchy on the camp; Hawkeye even lovingly called him "Dad" sometimes. Though bureaucracy continued to frustrate, the older man, unlike Henry, could wring results from the system. Under the Potter regime, the system seemed less at fault. Indeed, in addition to being a fine doctor and a knowing counselor, Col. Potter seemed like just what the hospital, the army, and, perhaps by unwitting implication, the Vietnam War had needed all along: a competent administrator. Such portrayals were a far cry from those in which we could take pleasure in Henry Blake's "unfitness for command," when being the best possible healer meant keeping military strictures and customs at arm's length.

Though it may come as a surprise to *MASH* viewers, Dr. H. Richard Hornberger was a staunch conservative who said he was frequently put off by the show's snickers at American patriotism and swipes at the military. He claimed to be a big fan of the Altman film, however, and saw it several times in its original release—a puzzling disparity in that the movie was more archly antimilitary than the TV version. Dr. Hornberger's divided sensibilities might be taken as emblematic of the national reaction to the weekly *MASH*.

MASH's final installment, "Good-bye, Farewell, and Amen," duly noted that the machinery was in motion to involve the United States in Vietnam even before the Korean War ended. Yet by 1983, when a puzzled Cpl. Klinger asked, "Where's Indochina?" upon hearing news of American support for anticommunist forces there, the question might have been coming from those too young to remember or those already disregarding the lessons of Vietnam at the crest of Reagan's "Morning in America." The disastrous deaths of hundreds of marines in Beirut and the dubious "liberation" of Grenada were only a few months away. [*MASH* writer] Larry Gelbart later observed that *MASH*'s longevity may finally have defeated its original intentions, saying to the audience in effect that war isn't so bad: "Given the right buddies, and the right CO, and the right kind of sense of humor, you can muddle through."

5

America Since Vietnam: War Makes a Comeback

Star Wars and America's Response to Vietnam

Tom Engelhardt

In 1977, given the apparent war-weary mood of the nation in the wake of Vietnam, it is surprising that even a fantasy film about war could be as popular as George Lucas's *Star Wars* proved to be. *Star Wars* was a hit with audiences because it provided a vision of war that was in many ways the opposite of Vietnam. In Vietnam, U.S. soldiers had massacred civilians at the village of My Lai; in *Star Wars* it is the protagonist, Luke Skywalker, who sees his own family massacred by enemy troops. Americans had been appalled at the harsh conditions and high casualty rates in Vietnam, but in *Star Wars* war was sleek, technological, and bloodless. *Star Wars* made "playing war" once again an acceptable activity for children. The film's success indicates that Americans were not tired of war as much as they were tired of the Vietnam War.

Tom Engelhardt is consulting editor at Metropolitan Books and coeditor of *History Wars: The Enola Gay and Other Battles for the American Past*. The following is an excerpt from his book *The End of Victory Culture: Cold War America and the Disillusioning of a Generation*.

NOW THAT DARTH VADER'S BREATHY TECHNO-voice is a staple of our culture, it's hard to remember how

■

Excerpted from *The End of Victory Culture: Cold War America and the Disillusionment of a Generation*, by Tom Engelhardt (New York: Basic Books, 1995). Reprinted by permission of the Elaine Markson Literary Agency, Inc., as agent for the author.

empty was the particular sector of space *Star Wars* blasted into. The very day the Paris Peace Accords were signed in 1973, Richard Nixon also signed a decree ending the draft. It was an admission of the obvious: war, American-style, had lost its hold on young minds. As an activity, it was now to be officially turned over to the poor and nonwhite.

Rescuing War Stories

Those in a position to produce movies, TV shows, comics, novels, or memoirs about Vietnam were convinced that Americans felt badly enough without such reminders. It was simpler to consider the war film and war toy casualties of Vietnam than to create cultural products with the wrong heroes, victims, and villains. In *Star Wars*, Lucas successfully challenged this view, decontaminating war of its recent history through a series of inspired cinematic decisions that rescued crucial material from the wreckage of Vietnam. To start with, he embraced the storylessness of the period, creating his own self-enclosed universe in deepest space and in an amorphous movie past, "a long time ago in a galaxy far, far away." Beginning with "Episode IV" of a projected nonology, he offered only the flimsiest of historical frameworks—an era of civil war, an evil empire, rebels, an ultimate weapon, a struggle for freedom.

Mobilizing a new world of special effects and computer graphics, he then made the high-tech weaponry of the recent war exotic, bloodless, and sleekly unrecognizable. At the same time, he uncoupled the audience from a legacy of massacre and atrocity. The blond, young Luke Skywalker is barely introduced before his adoptive family—high-tech peasants on an obscure planet—suffers its own My Lai. Imperial storm troopers led by Darth Vader descend upon their homestead and turn it into a smoking ruin (thus returning fire to its rightful owners). Luke—and the audience—can now set off on an anti-imperial venture as the victimized, not as victimizers. Others in space will torture, maim, and destroy. Others will put "us" in high-tech tiger cages; and our revenge, whatever it may be, will be justified.

Good-Guy Rebels

In this way, *Star Wars* denied the enemy a role "they" had monopolized for a decade—that of brave rebel. It was the first cultural product to ask of recent history, "Hey! How come *they* got all the fun?" And to respond, "Let's give them the burden of empire! Let's bog them down and be the plucky underdogs ourselves!"

Like Green Berets or Peace Corps members, Lucas's white teenage rebels would glide effortlessly among the natives. They would learn from value-superior Third World mystics like the Ho-Chi-Minh-ish Yoda in *The Empire Strikes Back* and be protected by ecological fuzzballs like the Ewoks in *Return of the Jedi*. In deepest space, anything was possible, including returning history to its previous owners. Once again, we could have it all: freedom *and* victory, captivity *and* rescue, underdog status *and* the spectacle of slaughter. As with the Indian fighter of old, advanced weaponry *and* the spiritual powers of the guerrilla might be ours.

Left to the enemy would be a Nazi-like capacity for destroying life, a desire to perform search-and-destroy missions on the universe, and the breathy machine voice of Darth Vader (as if evil were a dirty phone call from the Darkside). The Tao of the Chinese, the "life force" of Yaqui mystic Don Juan, even the political will of the Vietnamese would rally to "our" side as the Force and be applied to a crucial technical problem; for having the Force "with you" meant learning to merge with your high-tech weaponry in such a way as to assure the enemy's destruction. Looked at today, the last part of *Star Wars* concentrates on a problem that might have been invented after, not fourteen years before, the 1991 Persian Gulf War: how to fly a computerized, one-man jet fighter down a narrow corridor under heavy antiaircraft fire and drop a missile into an impossibly small air shaft, the sole vulnerable spot in the Emperor's Death Star.

High-Tech War

Here, Lucas even appropriated the kamikaze-like fusion of human and machine. In Vietnam, there had been two such man-machine meldings. The first, the bombing campaign, had the machinelike impersonality of the production line. Lifting off from distant spots of relative comfort like Guam, B-52 crews delivered their bombs to coordinates stripped of place or people and left the war zone for another day. The crew member symbolically regained humanity only when the enemy's technology stripped him of his machinery—and, alone, he fluttered to earth and captivity. At the same time, from Secretary of Defense McNamara's "electronic battlefield" to the first "smart bombs," Vietnam proved an experimental testing ground for machine-guided war. Unlike the B-52 or napalm, the smart bomb, the computer, the electronic sensor, and the video camera were not discredited by the war; and it was these machines of wonder that Lucas rescued through the innocence of special effects.

In James Bond films, high-tech had been a display category like fine wines, and techno-weaponry just another consumer item for 007. For Lucas, however, technology in the right hands actually solved problems, offering—whether as laser sword or X-wing fighter—not status but potential spiritualization. This elevation of technology made possible the return of slaughter to the screen as a triumphal and cleansing pleasure (especially since dying "imperial storm troopers," encased in full body carapaces, looked like so many bugs).

Reviving the War Toy Industry

Not only would George Lucas put "war" back into a movie title, he would almost single-handedly reconstitute war play as a feel-good activity for children. With G.I. Joe's demise, the world of child-sized war play stood empty. The toy soldier had long ago moved into history, an object for adult collectors. However, some months before *Star Wars* opened, Fox reached an agreement with Kenner Products, a toy company, to create action figures and fantasy vehicles geared to the movie. Kenner president Bernard Loomis decided that these would be inexpensive, new-style figures, only 3¾-inch high. Each design was to be approved by Lucas himself.

Since Kenner could not produce the figures quickly enough for the 1977 Christmas season, Loomis offered an "Early Bird Certificate Package"—essentially an empty box— that promised the child the first four figures when produced. The result was toy history. In 1978, Kenner sold over 26 million figures; by 1985, 250 million. All 111 figures and other *Star Wars* paraphernalia, ranging from lunch boxes and watches to video games, would ring up $2.5 billion in sales.

By the early 1980s, children's TV had become a *Star Wars*–like battle zone. Outnumbered rebels daily transformed themselves from teenagers into mighty robots "loved by good, feared by evil" (*Voltron*) or "heroic teams of armed machines" (*M.A.S.K.*) in order to fight Lotar and his evil, blue-faced father from Planet Doom (*Voltron*), General Spidrax, master of the Dark Domain's mighty armies (*Sectaurs*), or the evil red-eyed Darkseid of the Planet Apokolips (*Superfriends*).

Future war would be a machine-versus-machine affair, a bloodless matter of special effects, in the revamped war story designed for childhood consumption. In popular cartoons like *Transformers*, where good "Autobots" fought evil "Decepticons," Japanese-animated machines transformed themselves from mundane vehicles into futuristic weapons systems. At the same time, proliferating teams of action figures, *Star Wars*–size and linked to such shows, were transported into millions of homes where new-style war scenarios could be played out. . . .

Politicians Follow *Star Wars*'s Lead

It took some time for political leaders to catch up with George Lucas's battle scenarios. In the years when he was producing *Star Wars*, America's post-Vietnam presidents were having a woeful time organizing any narrative at all. In the real world, there seemed to be no Lucas-like outer space into which to escape the deconstruction job Vietnam had done to the war story. The military was in shambles; the public, according to pollsters, had become resistant to American troops being sent into battle anywhere; and past enemies were now negotiating partners in a new "détente."

Gerald Ford, inheriting a collapsed presidency from Richard Nixon, attempted only once to display American military resolve. In May 1975, a month after Saigon fell, Cambodian Khmer Rouge rebels captured an American merchant ship, the *Mayaguez*. Ford ordered the bombing of the Cambodian port city of Kampong Son and sent in the marines. They promptly stormed an island on which the *Mayaguez* crew was not being held, hours after ship and crew had been released, and fought a pointless, bitter battle, suffering forty-one dead. The event seemed to mock American prowess, confirming that rescue, like victory, had slipped from its grasp.

Jimmy Carter, elected president in 1976, had an even more woeful time of it. Facing what he termed a Vietnam-induced "national malaise," he proposed briefly that Americans engage in "the moral equivalent of war" by mobilizing and sacrificing on the home front to achieve energy independence from the OPEC oil cartel. The public, deep in a peacetime recession, responded without enthusiasm. In 1979, in a defining moment of his presidency, Carter watched helplessly as young Islamic followers of the Iranian Ayatollah Khomeini took fifty-two Americans captive in the U.S. embassy in Teheran and held them for 444 days. In April 1980, "Desert One," a military raid the president ordered to rescue the captives, failed dismally in the Iranian desert, and the president was forced to live out his term against a televised backdrop of unending captivity and humiliation that seemed to highlight American impotence.

Only with the presidency of Ronald Reagan did a Lucas-like reconstitution of the war story truly begin at the governmental level. The new president defined the Soviet Union in *Star Wars*–like terms as an "evil empire," while the army began advertising for recruits on TV by displaying spacy weaponry and extolling the pleasures of being "out there" in search of "the bad guys." In Nicaragua, Angola, Afghanistan, and elsewhere, the Reagan administration managed to portray the forces it supported as outnumbered "freedom fighters" struggling to roll back an overwhelming tide of imperial evil. This time, we would do the hitting and running, and yet we—or our surrogates—would retain the high-tech weaponry: mines for their harbors and Stinger missiles for their helicopters. Meanwhile, planners discovered in an intervention in Grenada that, with the right media controls in place and speed, you could produce the equivalent of an outer space war fantasy here on earth. No wonder that a group of junior officers at the Army Command and General Staff College at Fort Leavenworth responsible for aspects of the ground campaign used against Iraq in 1991 would be nicknamed the Jedi Knights.

Rambo and the New Patriotism in 1980s Action Films

Terry Christensen

Americans elected Ronald Reagan to the presidency in 1980 in part because he promised to restore the nation's international prestige and military prowess. The renewed patriotism that accompanied Reagan's presidency is reflected in action films of the 1980s, many of which dealt with Cold War and Vietnam themes. In *Red Dawn*, average Americans fend off a Soviet invasion, and in *Rocky IV* the U.S.-Soviet rivalry is played out in a boxing ring. The film *Rambo* deals with a mission to return to Vietnam to rescue prisoners of war. At the beginning of the film, Rambo sarcastically asks, "Do we get to win this time?" With few exceptions, in the action films of the 1980s the answer to that question was a resounding yes.

Terry Christensen is a professor of political science at San Jose State University. He is the author of *Reel Politics: American Political Movies from* Birth of a Nation *to* Platoon, from which the following essay is excerpted.

MOVIES CRITICAL OF AMERICAN FOREIGN POLICY were made throughout the Reagan years and some were popular successes, but the era will be remembered for a very different sort of film. Like President Reagan himself, these movies called up traditional values, emphasizing individual-

■

ism, self-sufficiency, competition, courage, pride, and patriotism in a conveniently simplified world. The American voters expressed their longing for a return to these values when they elected Ronald Reagan in 1980. They wanted a president who was sure of himself and his nation, unbothered by doubt, and unfazed by the complexities of the nation, the world, or human behavior.

People liked Reagan himself even more than they liked his policies. They were often willing to overlook his political shortcomings because of his congeniality and his communication skills. Worries about his lack of experience in foreign affairs were soon swept away by an almost unprecedented wave of patriotic fervor. The joyous return of the Iranian hostages on the day of Reagan's inauguration launched the revival of American pride and patriotism.

Reagan called for a renewal of American power and boosted the nation's military might with massive increases in defense spending. Suddenly the cold war was back, and so was interventionism. Reagan bombed Beirut, sent troops into Lebanon, and loosed the U.S. Marines on the tiny island of Grenada. He intervened cautiously but decisively in El Salvador, propping up a right-wing regime, then pushing it to elections and modest reform. It was too late for such action in Nicaragua, so Reagan isolated that nation economically and backed the Contra counterrevolutionaries. Later on, Reagan sent U.S. jets to raid Libya, which he claimed was the headquarters of world terrorism. Much of America loved every bit of it. Nearly six years of self-congratulation culminated in the 1986 rededication of the Statue of Liberty, an orgy of patriotism produced in the lavish style of a Hollywood movie. And much of this patriotic frenzy is reflected in a group of films produced during Reagan's presidency.

A New Cold War and New Patriotism

Reaganite movies didn't come into their own until after the 1984 reelection, but the trend started in 1982 with Sylvester Stallone's *First Blood*, for which the *Rocky* movies and *F.I.S.T.* had paved the way. John Rambo (Stallone), a former Green Beret and winner of the Congressional Medal of Honor, is an alienated and itinerant Vietnam vet searching for a buddy who survived the war. After learning that his friend has died of Agent Orange–induced cancer, the distraught Rambo wanders around, looking like a cross between a hippie and a Hell's Angel. Not surprisingly, a small town sheriff (Brian Dennehy) orders him to move on and drives him to the outskirts of town. Rambo, who does not like being told what to do, starts back into town. The two men fight, and Rambo is arrested. In jail, he becomes a victim of police brutality. With visions of Vietnam in his head, Rambo goes berserk and breaks out, fleeing to the woods.

A posse pursues Rambo. The most brutal deputy dies when he goes too far, but Rambo only wounds the rest, declaring, "Out here I'm the law!" Supplemented by the National Guard and state police, the posse traps Rambo. The pursuers think he's dead, but he's only angry. Resurrected, he

The 1984 Invasion of Grenada: A Very Popular Little War

Reagan, a man who, above all else, understood the value of appearance, promised the public that, after so many years of seeming weakness, his main goal would be to help make "America stand tall again." Promises made are not always promises kept, unfortunately. . . . In October 1983, a suicide bomber drove a truck loaded with explosives into the Marine compound [in Beirut]; the resulting explosion killed 241 Americans and wounded an additional 80 more. When the president announced some weeks after this debacle that all American troops would be placed on warships off the coast, it was hard to argue that the nation was "standing tall."

At the point where things seemed the bleakest (and with a presidential election looming for 1984), the possibility of diverting the public's attention by beginning a military conquest became a reality. On the small West Indian island of Grenada, a communist-leaning government had negotiated a number of agreements with various Eastern bloc countries. When, in mid-1983, a radical, militar-

chases the nasty sheriff to his headquarters and kills him. His old Green Beret commander (Richard Crenna) tries to talk the surrounded Rambo into surrendering. "Do you want a war you can't win?" he asks.

"They drew first blood," Rambo replies, "not me," at long last explaining himself. "It wasn't my war. You asked me, I didn't ask you. And I did what I had to do to win, but somebody wouldn't let us win. And I come back to the world, and I see all those maggots at the airport, protesting me, calling me a baby-killer and all kinds of vile crap. Who are they to protest me, huh? Back there I could fly a gunship, I could drive a tank. I was in charge of million dollar equipment. Back here I can't even hold a job."

First Blood condemned the maltreatment of Vietnam vets, a message with which few would disagree, but the real point of

---

ily controlled council took over that tiny nation-state, Reagan decided to intervene. More than 1,900 army paratroopers and Marines were ordered to invade Grenada, depose the ruling junta, and (officially at least) rescue a handful of American students who were enrolled in the island's lone medical college. The invasion was a total success—a great "victory" according to administration spokespersons—and many Americans, rightly or wrongly, had a sense of pride at how easily the nation's might had triumphed. Though the UN General Assembly condemned the American action and many persons wondered if it did not signal a return to the "gunboat diplomacy" of the Wilson, Harding, and Coolidge administrations earlier in the century, the "war" was popular throughout the United States. The Clint Eastwood film *Heartbreak Ridge*, one of the few motion pictures to look at the invasion, reemphasized that feeling as it contrasted the life and times of a "defeated" Marine veteran from Vietnam who now was able to train and bring the young troops under his command to total victory over the enemy.

M. Paul Holsinger, ed., *War and American Popular Culture*, 1999.

this film was action. Although critics laughed at the movie, Stallone laughed last: *First Blood* was a box office smash, and he followed it with a dumber movie that was an even bigger hit.

The next Reaganite movie was *Red Dawn*, directed by John Milius, the author of *Apocalypse Now*. It is the story of a small Colorado town that is invaded by Russian, Cuban, and Nicaraguan communists. The Wolverines, a group of teenagers who resemble the partisans in World War II movies, resist the attackers. Politicians are represented by the mayor of the town, who collaborates with the communists. The teenagers run rings around the occupying army for a while, but in the end they sacrifice themselves in a kamikaze-style mission. The movie closes with a shot of "Partisan Rock," a monument to the heroes of the resistance.

"Movies like *Red Dawn* are rapidly preparing America for World War III," said the chairman of the National Coalition on Television Violence, denouncing its 134 acts of violence per hour and labelling it "the most violent film ever seen."[1] Dismissed by critics as a mediocre action movie, *Red Dawn* was nevertheless a box office hit: it made $10 million in its first five days in release. "The ferocity of the American people," director John Milius smugly observed, "has always been underestimated."[2] Certainly the popularity of his film was due to its action rather than its politics. *Red Dawn* was anti-communist, but only because communists were convenient enemies; the bad guys had no perceivable political ideology and could just as easily have been from outer space. The inclusion of Latinos among the invaders distinguished *Red Dawn* from the anti-communist movies of the 1950s, but otherwise it was no more politically sophisticated. Indeed, it was more rabidly individualistic than anti-communist.

Although it was hard to take the politics of *Red Dawn* seriously, the movie did set precedents that other films would soon follow. It revived communists as convenient enemies, and it proved the marketability of posturing patriots as heroes. Few movies had fallen back on these old stereotypes since the fifties. After the Cuban missile confrontation in the early sixties, America and the Soviet Union moved toward detente, and so did the movies. Superpatriot heroes and communist villains went out of style and stayed out during the cynical sixties and seventies, when movies like *The Spy Who Came in from the Cold* and *Dr. Strangelove* were more common than films like *The Green Berets*. But in the eighties, the public response to Ronald Reagan made patriotism and anti-communism okay again, and *Red Dawn* proved they were good box office.

Once unleashed, Reaganite cinema became even cruder. *First Blood* and *Red Dawn* looked sophisticated compared to what followed. *Missing in Action* (1984) and *Invasion U.S.A.* (1985) were raw action flicks starring Chuck Norris, a wooden actor whose gift for stunt work presumably accounts for his great popularity. In *Missing in Action*, Norris plays an escaped prisoner of war who returns to Vietnam with an American senator who is investigating allegations about American soldiers "missing in action" (MIAs). Discredited by the evil Vietnamese and disowned by the American politician, the hero wreaks havoc on various enemy encampments, prisons, and convoys, saves the MIAs, and brings them back to Ho Chi Minh City to repudiate the Vietnamese liars. "You guys are going home," he assures the MIAs. Quite rightly, critics didn't take *Missing in Action* seriously. Like other Chuck Norris movies, however, it did well at the box office, despite its lack of tension, credibility, and excitement.

In Norris's other box office hit, *Invasion U.S.A.*, he plays an ex-CIA agent who comes out of retirement to stop a Russian "invasion" of Florida. This invasion might more accurately have been called a terrorist infiltration, but that wouldn't have made as good a title. Diabolical communists in various disguises slaughter Cuban refugees, ghetto dwellers, Christmas shoppers, and families in suburban homes, stirring up distrust and unrest and turning people against one another. "America has not been invaded by a foreign enemy in nearly two hundred years," the communist villain sneers. "Look at them . . . soft, spineless, decadent. They don't even understand the nature of their own freedom or how we will use it against them. They are their own worst enemies, but they don't know it." The movie confirms this analysis when cowardly FBI agents phone in sick and spoiled citizens whine about rationing. The "tide of terror" turns into a "threat to democracy," with demands for martial law and the suspension of the Constitution, but happily, the hero stops the invaders single-handedly.

Thanks in part to a larger budget, *Invasion U.S.A.* was better than *Missing in Action*, although neither of Norris's popular movies had much to say about politics. International tensions were merely an excuse for violent action, feeding Reaganite anti-communism. More seriously, *Missing in Action* cheaply exploited a subject that genuinely worried some Americans.

The Return of *Rambo*

Rambo's return was almost as crude, but *Rambo: First Blood Part II* (1985), written by Sylvester Stallone, was even more popular than the Reaganite movies that preceded it. John Rambo (Stallone again) wins a pardon for his earlier rampage in the woods when he accepts an assignment to find American MIAs in Vietnam. "Do we get to win this time?" Rambo asks his former Green Beret commander (Richard Crenna). He's only supposed to photograph the MIAs for evidence, but he tries to bring one back. The helicopter sent to pick him up abandons them, and the Vietnamese and their Russian advisers capture and torture Rambo. He escapes, slaughters the enemy, frees the MIAs, and leads—or drags—them to safety. He trashes the headquarters of the U.S. mission when he gets back and warns its bureaucratic chief to find the rest of the MIAs or risk the wrath of Rambo. This movie places the blame for the MIAs' continued captivity squarely on the U.S. government, which first declined to win the war and then refused to pay war reparations to Vietnam in exchange for the MIAs.

In a promotion video for *Rambo*, Stallone, unlike most filmmakers, was forthright in declaring his movie political. "I hope to establish a character that can represent a certain section of the American consciousness," he said, "and through the entertainment [I also hope to] be educational. . . . More than being just a fighting man, [Rambo] represents the entire fighting force." Stallone also claimed his movie was part of the "pre-stages of a true historical event" in which the existence of the MIAs would be verified. "It's no big secret," he declared. "Vietnam wants reparations from us. We don't want to pay all those billions," possibly because "our officials are being paid off." Movies like *Rambo* were popular, Stallone asserted, "because the people are on to something. There's a thirst for verification."[3]

Despite derisive reviews and Stallone's pretensions, *Rambo* was a big hit, even though the action was facile and without tension. *First Blood* was a better action film because of more skillful direction and because Rambo's white antagonists were not reduced to racist stereotypes, which may also be why *Invasion U.S.A.* had more tension than *Missing in Action*. David Morell, the author of the novel on which *First Blood* was based, dismissed *Rambo* as "a cartoon. On military bases," Morell said, "they show it as a comedy."[4] Others took it more seriously, though few critics liked it. David Halberstram labeled Stallone "a cinematic Joseph McCarthy" for his assertions about the existence of the MIAs and for conveying the "exact reverse of the real message of the Vietnam War."[5] President Ronald Reagan, on the other hand, admired Stallone's message. "After seeing *Rambo* last night," he joked during a terrorist crisis, "I know what to do next time this happens." He failed to comment on *Rambo*'s contention of U.S. government complacency in freeing the MIAs, however.

Anti-communism was also the theme of three other movies released in 1985: *Rocky IV, Eleni,* and *White Nights.* Stallone wrapped himself in the flag for his fourth Rocky film, in which the boxing hero comes out of retirement to defeat a Soviet fighter produced by biochemical engineering rather than old-fashioned hard work. The fight takes place in Moscow, where a hostile crowd of communists ends up cheering Rocky and he calls for international understanding in a concluding speech that attempts to mitigate the anti-communism of the rest of the film. *Eleni,* the true story of journalist Nicholas Gage's search for the communists who killed his mother in the Greek civil war, made no such gesture. "It is cartoon time even for the supposedly political cinema," wrote critic Andrew Sarris, "but *Eleni,* alas, doesn't work even as a cartoon."[6] It was the only one of the new cold war films to fail at the box office. *White Nights* was more successful thanks to the presence of Mikhail Baryshnikov and the direction of Taylor Hackford (*An Officer and a Gentleman*). An airliner makes an emergency landing in Soviet territory and a Russian ballet dancer (Baryshnikov) who has defected to the United States is taken captive. He escapes with a black American tap-dancer (Gregory Hines) who has defected to the Soviets. Director Hackford played down his movie's politics, claiming it was "only realistic about artistic freedom," but

Baryshnikov was more accurate when he said that "this film is politically right wing and patriotic."[7]

Iron Eagle, Heartbreak Ridge, and *Top Gun* (all 1986) soon added to what the Soviet press labeled "war-nography." In *Iron Eagle,* an American teenager flies to the rescue of his father, whose plane has been shot down over North Africa. The movie praises President Reagan as "this guy who don't take no shit from no gimpy country," but Reagan's government fails to save the captive pilot, forcing the teenager to do the job himself. *Heartbreak Ridge* featured a tough career soldier (Clint Eastwood) making men of his trainees, who are ultimately tested in the triumphant, if fanciful, invasion of Grenada.

Top Gun topped them both, though, at least at the box office, becoming the biggest ticket seller of 1986. Maverick (Tom Cruise), the young pilot who must become "top gun," is obsessed by the memory of his father, who was shot down under mysterious circumstances over Southeast Asia. It turns out that Dad was a hero, but details of his death have been kept secret for political reasons. Maverick ultimately proves himself in a skirmish with an unnamed enemy whose pilots fly MIGs. *Top Gun* takes such confrontations for granted, beginning with U.S. and enemy jets playing tag, and ending in real combat. Lest the audience worry that this incident might trigger World War III, we are told that "the other side denied the incident." The implication that this sort of thing is a daily occurrence is terrifying—all the more so because the U.S. Navy wholeheartedly endorsed and cooperated in the making of this picture. *Top Gun* is a throwback to old-fashioned war movies, no longer calling for calm vigilance, as did *Strategic Air Command* in 1955, but advocating confrontational machismo instead. Slick and shallow, it was the essence of Reaganite cinema.

Notes

1. *Stills,* 13 October 1984, p. 15.
2. Ibid.
3. *The Guardian,* 20 July 1985.
4. *Time Out,* 23–29 April 1986.
5. *California,* July 1986.
6. Village Voice, 5 November 1985.
7. Quoted in *People,* 16 December 1985.

Warrior Dreams: Paramilitary Culture in Post-Vietnam America

James William Gibson

The "action-adventure" genre of film—which features good men defeating bad men in armed combat—exploded in the 1980s, and since that time war and warriors have been increasingly celebrated in American culture. Other trends in popular entertainment, such as the success of authors such as Tom Clancy and his military thriller novels; the growth of warrior magazines such as *Soldier of Fortune;* rising sales of military-style weapons; and the emergence of the "hobby" of paintball, all point to a new "paramilitary culture" that has taken hold in America. These war fantasies can be understood partly as a national reaction to the Vietnam War, but also as a male reaction to the feminist movement of the 1960s and 1970s and the economic changes of the 1970s and 1980s. American men have sought escape from the realities of modern life by taking refuge in archaic warrior myths.

James William Gibson is a sociologist, historian, and the author of *The Perfect War: Technowar in Vietnam* and *Warrior Dreams: Paramilitary Culture in Post-Vietnam America*, from which the following selection is excerpted.

■

WE COULDN'T SEE THEM, BUT WE COULD HEAR their bugles sound the call. The Communist battalions were organizing for a predawn assault. Captain Kokalis smiled wickedly; he'd been through this before. A "human wave" assault composed of thousands of enemy soldiers was headed our way. The captain ordered the remaining soldiers in his command to check their .30- and .50-caliber machine guns. Earlier in the night, the demolitions squad attached to our unit had planted mines and explosive charges for hundreds of meters in front of our position.

And then it began. At a thousand meters, the soldiers emerged screaming from the gray-blue fog. "Fire!" yelled Captain Kokalis. The gun crews opened up with short bursts of three to seven rounds; their bullets struck meat. Everywhere I could see, clusters of Communist troops were falling by the second. But the wave still surged forward. At five hundred meters, Kokalis passed the word to his gunners to increase their rate of fire to longer strings of ten to twenty rounds. Sergeant Donovan, the demolitions squad leader, began to reap the harvest from the night's planting. Massive explosions ripped through the Communist troops. Fire and smoke blasted into the dawn sky. It was as if the human wave had hit a submerged reef; as the dying fell, wide gaps appeared in the line where casualties could no longer be replaced.

But still they kept coming, hundreds of men, each and every one bent on taking the American position and wiping us out. As the Communists reached one hundred meters, Kokalis gave one more command. Every machine gun in our platoon went to its maximum rate of sustained full-automatic frenzy, sounding like chain saws that just keep cutting and cutting.

And then it was over. The attack subsided into a flat sea of Communist dead. No Americans had been killed or wounded. We were happy to be alive, proud of our victory. We only wondered if our ears would ever stop ringing and if we would ever again smell anything other than the bittersweet aroma of burning gunpowder. . . .

Although an astonishing triumph was achieved that day, no historian will ever find a record of this battle in the hundreds of volumes and thousands of official reports written about the Korean or Vietnam war. Nor was the blood spilt part of a covert operation in Afghanistan or some unnamed country in Africa, Asia, or Latin America.

No, this battle was fought inside the United States, a few miles north of Las Vegas, in September 1986. It was a purely *imaginary* battle, a dream of victory staged as part of the *Soldier of Fortune* magazine's annual convention. The audience of several hundred men, women, and children, together with reporters and a camera crew from CBS News, sat in bleachers behind half a dozen medium and heavy machine guns owned by civilians. Peter G. Kokalis, *SOF*'s firearms editor, set the scene for the audience and asked them to imagine that the sandy brushland of the Desert Sportsman Rifle and Pistol Club was really a killing zone for incoming Communist troops. Kokalis was a seasoned storyteller; he'd given this performance before. When the fantasy battle was over, the fans went wild with applause. Kokalis picked up a microphone, praised Donovan (another *SOF* staff member)—"He was responsible for that whole damn Communist bunker that went up"—and told the parents in the audience to buy "claymores [antipersonnel land mines] and other good shit for the kids." A marvelous actor who knew what his audience wanted, Kokalis sneered, "Did you get that, CBS, on your videocam? Screw you knee-jerk liberals."

The shoot-out and victory over Communist forces conducted at the Desert Sportsman Rifle and Pistol Club was but one battle in a cultural or imaginary "New War" that had been going on since the late 1960s and early 1970s. The bitter controversies surrounding the Vietnam War had discredited the old American ideal of the masculine warrior hero for much of the public. But in 1971, when Clint Eastwood made the transition from playing cowboys in old *Rawhide* reruns and spaghetti westerns to portraying San Francisco police detective Harry Callahan in *Dirty Harry*, the warrior hero returned in full force. His backup arrived in 1974 when Charles Bronson appeared in *Death Wish*, the story of a mild-mannered, middle-aged architect in New York City who, after his wife is murdered and his daughter is raped and driven insane, finds new meaning in life through an endless war of revenge against street punks.

In the 1980s, Rambo and his friends made their assault.

The experience of John Rambo, a former Green Beret, was the paradigmatic story of the decade. In *First Blood* (1982), he burns down a small Oregon town while suffering hallucinatory flashbacks to his service in Vietnam. Three years later, in *Rambo: First Blood, Part 2*, he is taken off a prison chain gang by his former commanding officer in Vietnam and asked to perform a special reconnaissance mission to find suspected American POWs in Laos, in exchange for a Presidential pardon. His only question: "Do we get to win this time?" And indeed, Rambo does win. Betrayed by the CIA bureaucrat in charge of the mission, Rambo fights the Russians and Vietnamese by himself and brings the POWs back home.

Hundreds of similar films celebrating the victory of good men over bad through armed combat were made during the late 1970s and 1980s. Many were directed by major Hollywood directors and starred well-known actors. Elaborate special effects and exotic film locations added tens of millions to production costs. And for every large-budget film, there were scores of cheaper formula films employing lesser-known actors and production crews. Often these "action-adventure" films had only brief theatrical releases in major markets. Instead, they made their money in smaller cities and towns, in sales to Europe and the Third World, and most of all, in the sale of videocassettes to rental stores. Movie producers could even turn a profit on "video-only" releases; action-adventure films were the largest category of video rentals in the 1980s.

At the same time, Tom Clancy became a star in the publishing world. His book *The Hunt for Red October* (1984) told the story of the Soviet Navy's most erudite submarine commander, Captain Markus Ramius, and his effort to defect to the United States with the Soviets' premier missile-firing submarine. *Red Storm Rising* (1986) followed, an epic of World War III framed as a high-tech conventional war against the Soviet Union. Clancy's novels all featured Jack Ryan, Ph.D., a former Marine captain in Vietnam turned academic naval historian who returns to duty as a CIA analyst and repeatedly stumbles into life-and-death struggles in which the fate of the world rests on his prowess. All were bestsellers.

President Reagan, Secretary of the Navy John Lehman, and many other high officials applauded Clancy and his hero.

Soon the author had a multimillion-dollar contract for a whole series of novels, movie deals with Paramount, and a new part-time job as a foreign-policy expert writing op-ed pieces for the *Washington Post*, the *Los Angeles Times*, and other influential newspapers around the country. His success motivated dozens of authors, mostly active-duty or retired military men, to take up the genre. The "techno-thriller" was born.

At a slightly lower level in the literary establishment, the same publishing houses that marketed women's romance novels on grocery and drugstore paperback racks rapidly expanded their collections of pulp fiction for men. Most were written like hard-core pornography, except that inch-by-inch descriptions of penises entering vaginas were replaced by equally graphic portrayals of bullets, grenade fragments, and knives shredding flesh: "He tried to grab the handle of the commando knife, but the terrorist pushed down on the butt, raised the point and yanked the knife upward through the muscle tissue and guts. It ripped intestines, spilling blood and gore." A minimum of 20 but sometimes as many as 120 such graphically described killings occurred in each 200-to-250-page paperback. Most series came out four times a year with domestic print runs of 60,000 to 250,000 copies. More than a dozen different comic books with tides like *Punisher*, *Vigilante*, and *Scout* followed suit with clones of the novels.

Along with the novels and comics came a new kind of periodical which replaced the older adventure magazines for men, such as *True* and *Argosy*, that had folded in the 1960s. Robert K. Brown, a former captain in the U.S. Army Special Forces during the Vietnam War, founded *Soldier of Fortune: The Journal of Professional Adventurers* in the spring of 1975, just before the fall of Saigon. *SOF*'s position was explicit from the start: the independent warrior must step in to fill the dangerous void created by the American failure in Vietnam. By the mid-1980s *SOF* was reaching 35,000 subscribers, had newsstand sales of another 150,000, and was being passed around to at least twice as many readers.

Half a dozen new warrior magazines soon entered the market. Some, like *Eagle*, *New Breed*, and *Gung-Ho*, tried to copy the *SOF* editorial package—a strategy that ultimately failed. But most developed their own particular pitch. *Combat*

Handguns focused on pistols for would-be gunfighters. *American Survival Guide* advertised and reviewed everything needed for "the good life" after the end of civilization (except birth control devices—too many Mormon subscribers, the editor said), while *S.W.A.T.* found its way to men who idealized these elite police teams and who were worried about home defense against "multiple intruders."

During the same period, sales of military weapons took off. Colt offered two semiautomatic versions of the M16 used by U.S. soldiers in Vietnam (a full-size rifle and a shorter-barreled carbine with collapsible stock). European armories exported their latest products, accompanied by sophisticated advertising campaigns in *SOF* and the more mainstream gun magazines. Israeli Defense Industries put a longer, 16-inch barrel on the Uzi submachine gun (to make it legal) and sold it as a semiautomatic carbine. And the Communist countries of Eastern Europe, together with the People's Republic of China, jumped into the market with the devil's own favorite hardware, the infamous AK47. The AK sold in the United States was the semiautomatic version of the assault rifle used by the victorious Communists in Vietnam and by all kinds of radical movements and terrorist organizations around the world. It retailed for $300 to $400, half the price of an Uzi or an AR-15; complete with three 30-round magazines, cleaning kit, and bayonet, it was truly a bargain.

To feed these hungry guns, munitions manufacturers packaged new "generic" brands of military ammo at discount prices, often selling them in cases of 500 or 1,000 rounds. New lines of aftermarket accessories offered parts for full-automatic conversions, improved flash-hiders, scopes, folding stocks, and scores of other goodies. In 1989, the U.S. Bureau of Alcohol, Tobacco and Firearms (ATF) estimated that two to three million military-style rifles had been sold in this country since the Vietnam War. The Bureau released these figures in response to the public outcry over a series of mass murders committed by psychotics armed with assault rifles.

But the Bureau's statistics tell only part of the story. In less than two decades, millions of American men had purchased combat rifles, pistols, and shotguns and begun training to fight their own personal wars. Elite combat shooting schools teaching the most modern techniques and often costing $500 to over $1,000 in tuition alone were attended not only by soldiers and police but by increasing numbers of civilians as well. Hundreds of new indoor pistol-shooting ranges opened for business in old warehouses and shopping malls around the country, locations ideal for city dwellers and suburbanites.

A new game of "tag" blurred the line between play and actual violence: men got the opportunity to hunt and shoot other men without killing them or risking death themselves. The National Survival Game was invented in 1981 by two old friends, one a screenwriter for the weight-lifting sagas that gave Arnold Schwarzenegger his first starring roles, and the other a former member of the Army's Long Range Reconnaissance Patrol (LRRP) in Vietnam. Later called paintball because it utilized guns firing balls of watercolor paint, by 1987 the game was being played by at least fifty thousand people (mostly men) each weekend on both outdoor and indoor battlefields scattered across the nation. Players wore hard-plastic face masks intended to resemble those of ancient tribal warriors and dressed from head to toe in camouflage clothes imported by specialty stores from military outfitters around the world. The object of the game was to capture the opposing team's flag, inflicting the highest possible body count along the way.

One major park out in the Mojave Desert seventy miles southeast of Los Angeles was named Sat Cong Village. *Sat Cong* is a slang Vietnamese phrase meaning "Kill Communists" that had been popularized by the CIA as part of its psychological-warfare program. Sat Cong Village employed an attractive Asian woman to rent the guns, sell the paintballs, and collect the twenty-dollar entrance fee. Players had their choice of playing fields: Vietnam, Cambodia, or Nicaragua. On the Nicaragua field, the owner built a full-size facsimile of the crashed C-47 cargo plane contracted by Lieutenant Colonel Oliver North to supply the contras. The scene even had three parachutes hanging from trees; the only thing missing was the sole survivor of the crash, Eugene Hasenfus.

The 1980s, then, saw the emergence of a highly energized culture of war and the warrior. For all its varied manifestations, a few common features stood out. The New War culture was not so much military as paramilitary. The new warrior hero was only occasionally portrayed as a member of a conventional military or law enforcement unit; typically, he fought alone or with a small, elite group of fellow warriors. Moreover, by separating the warrior from his traditional state-sanctioned occupations—policeman or soldier—the New War culture presented the warrior role as the ideal identity for *all* men. Bankers, professors, factory workers, and postal clerks could all transcend their regular stations in life and prepare for heroic battle against the enemies of society.

To many people, this new fascination with warriors and weapons seemed a terribly bad joke. The major newspapers and magazines that arbitrate what is to be taken seriously in American society scoffed at the attempts to resurrect the warrior hero. Movie critics were particularly disdainful of Stallone's Rambo films. *Rambo: First Blood, Part 2* was called "narcissistic jingoism" by *The New Yorker* and "hare-brained" by the *Wall Street Journal.* The *Washington Post* even intoned that "Sly's body looks fine. Now can't you come up with a workout for his soul?"

But in dismissing Rambo so quickly and contemptuously, commentators failed to notice the true significance of the emerging paramilitary culture. They missed the fact that quite a few people were not writing Rambo off as a complete joke; behind the Indian bandanna, necklace, and bulging muscles, a new culture hero affirmed such traditional American values as self-reliance, honesty, courage, and concern for fellow citizens. Rambo was a worker and a former enlisted man, not a smooth-talking professional. That so many seemingly well-to-do, sophisticated liberals hated him for both his politics and his uncouthness only added to his glory. Further, in their emphasis on Stallone's clownishness the commentators failed to see not only how widespread paramilitary culture had become but also its relation to the historical moment in which it arose.

Indeed, paramilitary culture can be understood only when it is placed in relation to the Vietnam War. America's failure to win that war was a truly profound blow. The nation's long, proud tradition of military victories, from the Revolutionary War through the century-long battles against the Indians to World Wars I and II, had finally come to an end. Politically, the defeat in Vietnam meant that the post–World War II era of overwhelming American political and military power in international affairs, the era that in 1945 *Time* magazine publisher Henry Luce had prophesied would be the "American Century," was over after only thirty years. No longer could U.S. diplomacy wield the big stick of military intervention as a ready threat—a significant part of the American public would no longer support such interventions, and the rest of the world knew it.

Moreover, besides eroding U.S. influence internationally, the defeat had subtle but serious effects on the American psyche. America has always celebrated war and the warrior. Our long, unbroken record of military victories has been crucially important both to the national identity and to the personal identity of many Americans—particularly men. The historian Richard Slotkin locates a primary "cultural archetype" of the nation in the story of a heroic warrior whose victories over the enemy symbolically affirm the country's fundamental goodness and power; we win our wars because, morally, we deserve to win. Clearly, the archetypical pattern Slotkin calls "regeneration through violence" was broken with the defeat in Vietnam. The result was a massive disjunction in American culture, a crisis of self-image: If Americans were no longer winners, then who were they?

This disruption of cultural identity was amplified by other social transformations. During the 1960s, the civil rights and ethnic pride movements won many victories in their challenges to racial oppression. Also, during the 1970s and 1980s, the United States experienced massive waves of immigration from Mexico, Central America, Vietnam, Cambodia, Korea, and Taiwan. Whites, no longer secure in their power abroad, also lost their unquestionable dominance at home; for the first time, many began to feel that they too were just another hyphenated ethnic group, the Anglo-Americans.

Extraordinary economic changes also marked the 1970s and 1980s. U.S. manufacturing strength declined substantially; staggering trade deficits with other countries and the chronic federal budget deficits shifted the United States from creditor to debtor nation. The post–World War II American Dream—which promised a combination of technological progress and social reforms, together with high employment rates, rising wages, widespread home ownership, and ever increasing consumer options—no longer seemed a likely prospect for the great majority. At the same time, the rise in crime rates, particularly because of drug abuse and its accompanying violence, made people feel more powerless than ever.

While the public world dominated by men seemed to come apart, the private world of family life also felt the shocks. The feminist movement challenged formerly exclusive male domains, not only in the labor market and in many areas of political and social life but in the home as well. Customary male behavior was no longer acceptable in either private relationships or public policy. Feminism was widely experienced by men as a profound threat to their identity. Men had to change, but to what? No one knew for sure what a "good man" was anymore.

It is hardly surprising, then, that American men—lacking confidence in the government and the economy, troubled by the changing relations between the sexes, uncertain of their identity or their future—began to *dream*, to fantasize about the powers and features of another kind of man who could retake and reorder the world. And the hero of all these dreams was the paramilitary warrior. In the New War he fights the battles of Vietnam a thousand times, each time winning decisively. Terrorists and drug dealers are blasted into oblivion. Illegal aliens inside the United States and the hordes of non-whites in the Third World are returned by force to their proper place. Women are revealed as dangerous temptresses who have to be mastered, avoided, or terminated.

Obviously these dreams represented a flight from the present and a rejection and denial of events of the preceding twenty years. But they also indicated a more profound and severe distress. The whole modern world was damned as unacceptable. Unable to find a rational way to face the tasks of rebuilding society and reinventing themselves, men instead sought refuge in myths from both America's frontier past and ancient times. Indeed, the fundamental narratives that shape paramilitary culture and its New War fantasies are often nothing but reinterpretations or reworkings of archaic warrior myths.

In ancient societies, the most important stories a people told about themselves concerned how the physical universe came into existence, how their ancestors first came to live in this universe, and how the gods, the universe, and society were related to one another. These cosmogonic, or creation, myths frequently posit a violent conflict between the good forces of order and the evil forces dedicated to the perpetuation of primordial chaos. After the war in which the gods defeat the evil ones, they establish the "sacred order," in which all of the society's most important values are fully embodied. Some creation myths focus primarily on the sacred order and on the deeds of the gods and goddesses in paradise. Other myths, however, focus on the battles between the heroes and villains that lead up to the founding. In these myths it is war and the warrior that are most sacred. American paramilitary culture borrows from both kinds of stories, but mostly from this second, more violent, type.

In either case, the presence, if not the outright predominance, of archaic male myths at the moment of crisis indicates just how far American men jumped psychically when faced with the declining power of their identities and organizations. The always-precarious balance in modern society between secular institutions and ways of thinking on the one hand and older patterns of belief informed by myth and ritual on the other tilted decisively in the direction of myth. The crisis revealed that at some deep, unconscious level these ancient male creation myths live on in the psyche of many men and that the images and tales from this mythic world of warriors and war still shape men's fantasies about who they are as men, their commitments to each other and to women, and their relationships to society and the state.

EPILOGUE

Debating Portrayals of War in Popular Culture: Two Interpretations of *Saving Private Ryan*

Saving Private Ryan Is a Pro-War Film

Howard Zinn

Director Steven Spielberg's World War II drama *Saving Private Ryan* was one of the highest-grossing films of 1998. The film was praised for its realistic portrayal of the D-Day invasion of Normandy, and many viewers and critics say it reminds today's generation of the enormous sacrifices made by the soldiers who fought World War II.

While the film accurately depicts the horrors of war, on the whole it sends the message that all the sacrifice and bloodshed of World War II were justified. Defeating Nazi Germany was a worthwhile goal, but war films like *Saving Private Ryan* send the message that war itself can be a noble endeavor. In the following viewpoint, Howard Zinn argues that this message is harmful. After the Allied victory in World War II, it took the disaster of the Vietnam War for Americans to once again face the horror, immorality, and futility of war. *Saving Private Ryan* seems set to rescue the idea of a "good war," and unfortunately Americans are eager to assist.

Howard Zinn is a professor of political science at Boston University and the author of *A People's History of the United States*.

LIKE SO MANY WORLD WAR II VETERANS (I COULD see them all around me in the theater audience), I was drawn to see *Saving Private Ryan*. I had volunteered for the Air Force

■

Reprinted from "*Private Ryan* Saves War," by Howard Zinn, *The Progressive*, October 1998, by permission of *The Progressive*.

at the age of twenty. After training as a bombardier, I went overseas with my crew to fly some of the last bombing missions of the European war.

My pilot was nineteen. My tailgunner was eighteen. Every death in *Saving Private Ryan* reminded me, as it must have reminded other veterans, of how lucky we were, we who survived. My two closest Air Force buddies who went through training with me and then on to other theaters (what a word, "theaters"!)—Joe Perry to Italy, Ed Plotkin to the Pacific—were killed in the last weeks of the war.

Glorifying Military Heroism

I watched *Private Ryan*'s extraordinarily photographed battle scenes, and I was thoroughly taken in. But when the movie was over, I realized that it was exactly that—I had been taken in. And I disliked the film intensely. I was angry at it because I did not want the suffering of men in war to be used—yes, exploited—in such a way as to revive what should be buried along with all those bodies in Arlington Cemetery: the glory of military heroism.

"The greatest war movie ever made," the film critics say about *Saving Private Ryan*. They are a disappointing lot, the film critics. They are excited, even exultant, about the brilliant cinematography, depicting the bloody chaos of the Omaha Beach landing. But they are pitifully superficial.

They fail (with a few honorable exceptions, such as Vincent Canby in *The New York Times* and Donald Murray in *The Boston Globe*) to ask the most important question: Will this film help persuade the next generation that such scenes must never occur again? Will it make clear that we must resist war, even if it is accompanied by the seductive speeches of political leaders saying that this latest war, unlike other bad wars we remember, will be another "good" one, like World War II?

The admiring critics of the movie give their own answer to that: It is a war movie, they say, not an anti-war movie.

Some viewers have asked how can anyone want to go to war after seeing such horror? But knowing the horrors of war has never been an obstacle to a quick build-up of war spirit by patriotic political speeches and an obsequious press.

All that bloodshed, all that pain, all those torn limbs and

exposed intestines will not deter a brave people from going to war. They just need to believe that the cause is just. They need to be told: It is a war to end all wars (Woodrow Wilson), or we need to stop Communism (Kennedy, Johnson, Nixon), or aggression must not go unpunished (Bush), or international terrorists have declared war on us (Clinton).

"The Good War"

In *Saving Private Ryan,* there is never any doubt that the cause is just. This is the good war. There is no need to say the words explicitly. The heartrending crosses in Arlington National Cemetery get the message across, loud and clear. And a benign General Marshall, front and back of the movie, quotes Abraham Lincoln's words of solace to a mother who has lost five sons in the Civil War. The audience is left with no choice but to conclude that this one—while it causes sorrow to a million mothers—is in a good cause.

Yes, getting rid of fascism was a good cause. But does that unquestionably make it a good war? The war corrupted us, did it not? The hate it engendered was not confined to Nazis.

We put Japanese families in concentration camps.

We killed huge numbers of innocent people—the word "atrocity" fits—in our bombings of Dresden, Hamburg, Tokyo, and finally Hiroshima and Nagasaki.

And when the war ended, we and our Allies began preparing for another war, this time with nuclear weapons, which, if used, would make Hitler's Holocaust look puny.

We can argue endlessly over whether there was an alternative in the short run, whether fascism could have been resisted without fifty million dead. But the long-term effect of World War II on our thinking was pernicious and deep. It made war—so thoroughly discredited by the senseless slaughter of World War I—noble once again. It enabled political leaders—whatever miserable adventure they would take us into, whatever mayhem they would wreak on other people (two million dead in Korea, at least that many in Southeast Asia, hundreds of thousands in Iraq) and on our own—-to invoke World War II as a model.

Communism supplanted Nazism as a reason for war, and when we could no longer point to Communism as a threat, a convenient enemy, like Saddam Hussein, could be compared to Hitler. Our leaders used glib analogies to justify immense suffering. The presumed absolute goodness of World War II created an aura of rightness around war itself (note the absence of a great movement of protest against the Korean War), which only an adventure as monstrously evil, as soaked in official lies as Vietnam, could dispel.

Saving Private Ryan Rescues the Good Name of War

Vietnam caused large numbers of Americans to question the enterprise of war itself. Now, *Saving Private Ryan*, aided by superb cinematographic technology, draws on our deep feeling for the GIs in order to rescue not just *Private Ryan* but the good name of war.

I will not be surprised if Spielberg gets an Academy Award. Did not Kissinger get a Nobel Prize? The committees that give prizes are, too often, bereft of social conscience. But we are not bound to honor their choices.

To refresh my memory, I watched the video of *All Quiet on the Western Front*. With no musical background, without the benefit of modern cinematography, without fields of corpses, with no pools of blood reddening the screen, that film conveyed the horror of warfare more powerfully than *Saving Private Ryan*. The one fleeting shot of two hands clutching barbed wire, the rest of the body gone, said it all.

In Spielberg's film, we see Tom Hanks gunned down, and it is sad. But it is a prosaic sadness compared to the death of the protagonist in Erich Remarque's story, as we watch a butterfly hover over a trench, and we see the hand of Lew Ayres reach out for it and go limp. We see no dead body, only that beautiful butterfly, and the reaching hand.

But more important, *All Quiet on the Western Front* does not dodge—as *Saving Private Ryan* does, as its gushing critics do—the issue of war. In it, war is not just horrible; it is futile. It is not inevitable; it is manufactured. Back home, commenting on the war, is no kindly General Marshall, quoting Lincoln, but prosperous men urging the soldiers, "On to Paris, boys! On to Paris!"

The boys in the trenches don't just discuss the battle; they discuss the war. They ask: Who is profiting? They propose: Hey, let's have the world's leaders get into an arena and fight it out themselves! They acknowledge: We have no quarrel with the boys on the other side of the barbed wire!

Our culture is in deep trouble when a film like *Saving Private Ryan* can pass by, like a military parade, with nothing but a shower of confetti and hurrahs for its color and grandeur.

Saving Private Ryan Is an Antiwar Film

Christopher Caldwell

The World War II drama *Saving Private Ryan* is set during the D-Day invasion of Normandy and deals with a platoon of soldiers who have been ordered to find another soldier, Private James Ryan. Ryan's three brothers have all died in the war, and as a gesture of sympathy toward their mother the Army General Staff has ordered the fourth brother home. The film deals with soldiers' mixed feelings about risking their lives in order to save Private Ryan.

The soldiers' mixed feelings may well represent director Steven Spielberg's views about war. While the film has been praised for its brutally realistic portrayal of on-the-ground combat, Spielberg does not support this war-is-hell motif with a broader message that the Allied cause is worth the soldiers' sacrifice. In terms of the plot, it's clear that Private Ryan is *not* worth the sacrifice of a whole platoon of soldiers. Metaphorically, then, the war itself is not "worth it" either.

Christopher Caldwell is senior editor of the *Weekly Standard*, a conservative political magazine.

THERE IS LITTLE DISAGREEMENT THAT STEVEN Spielberg's smash hit, *Saving Private Ryan*, which opened July 24, is a powerful and richly textured account of war. The story it tells, of a small unit hunting for a lost paratrooper in Nazi-occupied Normandy, has won unstinting praise for its simplicity and evocativeness, and the film's brilliantly realistic depic-

■

Excerpted from "Spielberg at War," by Christopher Caldwell, *Commentary*, October 1998. Reprinted with permission. All rights reserved.

tion of the D-Day invasion of Europe is by general consensus without parallel in movie history. Jay Carr of the *Boston Globe* called *Saving Private Ryan* "the war movie to end all war movies." To Stephen Hunter of the *Washington Post*, it is "simply the greatest war movie ever made, and one of the great American movies. In one stroke, it makes everything that came before . . . seem dated and unwatchable."

Pro-War or Anti-War?

Yet *Saving Private Ryan* has also stirred up a good deal of controversy. On one side are those reviewers, by far the majority, who have applauded it for reviving the classic war film—"classic" in the sense of heroic, patriotic, and refreshingly free of irony—after a long period in which Vietnam-era cynicism held sway. Thus, the *New York Times* critic, Vincent Canby, raved about the film and concluded with relief that "With *Saving Private Ryan*, war is good again." But then there are those who have interpreted it differently. Gene Siskel, who liked the movie very much, found it to be an "action-filled *anti*-war film" (emphasis added); so did John Podhoretz in the *Weekly Standard*, who liked it considerably less on that account. Richard Schickel of *Time* and Edward Rothstein, a cultural critic for the *New York Times*, both focused on the film's imagery to argue that, whatever its cinematic virtues or flaws, it hardly brings us back to the status quo ante Vietnam.

Is *Saving Private Ryan* all-American or cynical, pro-war or anti-war? Spielberg himself has been of little help in clearing up the matter. In a series of interviews since the film's release, he has shown himself of two minds. "War is not about glory," he said to one interviewer, and then, somewhat contradictorily, "I felt we needed to be truthful to do honor to those soldiers." He has described the film as a memorial, but has warned pre-teens against seeing it. More gnomically, when asked point-blank whether the movie was anti-war, he told the *New Yorker*'s Hendrik Hertzberg, "I think it's an anti-war film only in that, if you want to go to war after seeing this picture, then it's not an anti-war film."

There is, of course, a subtext to the controversy. Many of the complaints about the movie—particularly those arising from conservatives—are really complaints about Steven Spielberg. That is understandable. He is not just a great filmmaker but one of the most prominent liberal activists in the country, a close friend of President Clinton, and a generous donor to feminist, pro-choice, and civil-rights causes. It is therefore natural to look upon *Saving Private Ryan* as the pronouncement of Spielberg's and Clinton's generation—the Vietnam generation that had an opportunity to fight and did not—on the World War II generation of their fathers, that did. And it is hardly surprising that those anxious to protect the reputation of the latter would be reluctant to entrust it to the former.

But are the complaints valid? . . .

Attacks Against the Film

There has been a handful of quibbles about specific period details in *Saving Private Ryan:* captains, for instance, do not wear their helmet insignias into battle. But the only narrowly historical question that bears on the heart of the film is whether General George C. Marshall would have plausibly ordered the public-relations maneuver on which the plot hinges: sending a unit of soldiers out to rescue one man, on the grounds that his three brothers had already died in action. In this, Spielberg has been vindicated; as the military historian John Keegan notes, "The Pentagon did have a policy of withdrawing the last surviving son of a numerous family from combat." In *Band of Brothers* (1992), Stephen Ambrose followed a company of paratroopers in the weeks after D-Day. Among them was a Private Frederick Niland, one of whose brothers was missing in action and two more of whom had been killed; he was retrieved by a special unit sent on orders of the War Department. Spielberg has described the Niland episode as "the kernel of truth around which this morality play has been fictionalized."

Another line of attack against *Saving Private Ryan* is that, even if its period details are correct, the story itself undercuts any potentially patriotic message. For one thing, that story is rich in examples of cowardice and criminality. Particularly striking is the climactic battle scene when Corporal Upham, an unctuous figure who is writing a book about how soldiers "bond" in wartime, cowers in fright, unable to fire a single shot, and winds up costing the lives of several of the men with whom he himself has supposedly "bonded." Only when the battle is over does he execute a captured prisoner in cold blood—the very man whom, in an earlier scene, Upham has begged his captain to free.

But are we supposed to sympathize with this coward? In the course of his interviews, Spielberg made a remarkable statement about Upham: "He was me in the movie. That's how I would have been in war" from which Richard Grenier, writing in the *Washington Times*, concluded that Spielberg is "rather proud of his cowardice." But whatever the director may have meant by his comment about Upham, having a coward in a war movie no more makes it a brief for cowardice than having an apothecary in *Romeo and Juliet* makes it soft on drugs. One can admire bravery without claiming that everyone is brave, or without claiming unusual bravery for oneself. In any case, *Saving Private Ryan*, which Spielberg has also called "a tribute to veterans," does unquestionably admire their valor, possibly even because that valor was less than perfectly universal.

Horrifying Realism

A subtler point that some have made in this connection is that the sheer accumulation of horrifying detail in *Saving Private Ryan*—the limbs blown off, the guts falling out, the near-absolute randomness of the carnage, the relentlessness with which it is all forced upon us—stacks the emotional deck against war. In this case, the charge, which also amounts to a tribute to Spielberg's genius as a craftsman, has substance. But it is also a little unfair.

Although no one would ever accuse this movie of warmongering, there is no question that Spielberg considers World War II to have met the highest threshold for sending men into battle. Indeed, the few veterans who have criticized the amount of gore in the movie have faulted Spielberg not for deprecating the war itself or those who waged it but for lacking sufficient respect for the dead. Typical is Navy veteran David Horton, who wrote to the *Los Angeles Times*:

> There were tanks that some bright engineers thought would float in the current of the English Channel. Well, they leaked, as anyone with an ounce of common sense could have told them, and they sank like stones. There were soldiers inside those tanks, and they drowned. I don't need

some filmmaker's stylized, make-believe violence to tell me how horrible that death must have been.

Here at last we begin, somewhat obliquely, to approach the real issue at the heart of the dispute over *Saving Private Ryan*.

That war is hell is a truth universally acknowledged by those who have fought in it. Similarly, the violence, the brutality and the arbitrariness of battle have been a staple of many a novel and movie. This emphatically includes movies about World War II—the "good" war—and it includes movies made by people who were actually at the invasion of Normandy (Darryl Zanuck's *The Longest Day* and Sam Fuller's *The Big Red One*, for instance). There is even a tradition in World War II movies, from *They Were Expendable* to *A Bridge Too Far*, of viewing much of the carnage as senseless—a tradition whose traces can be seen in a strongly "patriotic" film like William Wellman's *Battleground* (1949), which Spielberg has frequently cited as an influence.

If, in other words, there is something innovative about Spielberg's treatment of war—and there is—it does not lie only in its unprecedented realism, or in the extent to which that realism inevitably makes war itself abhorrent. It lies somewhere else.

The Narrative of Civilization

In any war, there are two narratives: the narrative of civilization, which wages wars, justly or unjustly, for reasons of state and/or out of considerations of honor, and the on-the-ground narrative, which basically consists of men killing one another. There can be overlap between the two narratives. The statesmen who run the war may have real solicitude, personal as well as broadly moral, for the men fighting it. (Indeed, such an act of solicitude is the springboard for the plot of *Saving Private Ryan*.) And the soldiers on the ground may believe in the cause for which they are fighting. But very frequently the two narratives exist in hermetic isolation from each other—which means that for the men engaged in combat, the actual experience of war is often nothing more than a battle to the death, independent of right and wrong.

All war movies have been made by people living in civilization for people living in civilization. Spielberg's is no exception. What is new about it is that, as a battle film, it is purged of the context of civilization. "Mercifully," wrote Jay Carr in the *Boston Globe*, "there's never a single overview or big-picture shot here, never a scene with Ike or Montgomery standing at a map with a pointer, spelling it all out for us." Why this should be a mercy is unclear, but it is certainly true that *Saving Private Ryan* offers its viewers no perspective outside that of the day-to-day life of a GI grunt.

If, in most war movies, we are never completely overwhelmed by the almost incomprehensible violence of battle, it is because we are simultaneously being made to understand the reasons why the war is being fought (or, as in 1980s Vietnam movies, the reasons why the war should not have been fought). By contrast, *Saving Private Ryan* hardly so much as acknowledges the existence of this realm of public values. The soldiers' experience of war may not be altogether values-less, but it is exiled from the values that put them there in the first place.

"I wanted the audience in the arena, not sitting off to one side," Spielberg has said. "I didn't want to make something it was easy to look away from." He has succeeded. According to John Podhoretz, "Spielberg takes World War II, and, in the interest of paying tribute to the almost unimaginable sacrifices made by those who fought it, minimizes the war beyond recognition." Actually, one might put it the other way around: at least in terms of the on-the-ground narrative, Spielberg does not minimize World War II but rather maximizes it. In fact, it is exactly through this maximization of the soldiers' experience that he has managed to make their "unimaginable sacrifices" a little bit more imaginable.

The Film's Ambiguous Message

Still—and here is where Podhoretz's point has bite—that does not address the question of what Spielberg himself makes, or wants us to make, of the war's larger, civilizational, purposes. In the absence of Ike-with-a-pointer, the two short "framing" segments at the start and end of the film are just about all the politics we have to go on. In these, an aged Private Ryan returns to Normandy to look at the graves of his fallen comrades. Turning to his wife, he says: "Tell me I'm a good man. Tell me I've led a good life."

It is no doubt this ambiguous sentiment that has led some critics to conclude that Spielberg intends to restore us to a benign, uncomplicatedly pre-Vietnam view of American character—in Stephen Hunter's words, "*Saving Private Ryan* is probably the most conservative film of the decade"—while leading others to object that, as Edward Rothstein put it, the film fatally "privatizes patriotism" by divorcing it from its proper, political context. Citing Rothstein in the *Los Angeles Times*, the film historian Neal Gabler in effect split the difference between these two views. If, he wrote,

> the film falsifies the sentiments of the soldiers of that time by having them declare they are fighting only to get back home, when in reality the soldiers in that war were avowedly fighting to stop Adolf Hitler, then the sentiments are at least falsified in a good cause: to neutralize the nationalism that had divided us [over Vietnam] and to humanize our sense of duty.

"To humanize our sense of duty" is a fine capsule description of the morality that informs *Saving Private Ryan*. On a personal level, there is much to be said for it—as is attested in the film by the many acts of bravery and sheer dogged determination performed by its protagonists. And yet, once our sense of duty has been "humanized," what really are we left with? Spielberg's movie assumes that its audience knows the reasons why World War II was fought; but any such assumption is fraught with pitfalls. Absent Ike-with-a-pointer, in what way are we witnessing in this movie anything other than cold-blooded, nonsensical, mass murder? Absent Hitler, absent the Nazis, is it fair—to use a "humanized" term—that several brave American officers should die while the coward Upham, or Ryan himself for that matter, should live? Not to mention the deaths of a whole Higgins boat full of innocent American boys, perforated with bullets before they can even take a step forward.

Not Worth It

"Ryan better be worth it," says Captain Miller, the character played by Tom Hanks, when informed he has to take his men into German territory to find him. "He better go home and cure some disease or invent a new, longer-lasting lightbulb." But Ryan is not a medical pioneer, not an inventor. As a young man, he is so thick he does not even know what the word "context" means. As an old man, he is a thoroughly tacky and undistinguished-looking American tourist in a polyester windbreaker. These are the terms—the on-the-ground, soldier's-eye terms in which we see Private Ryan. In these terms, we know him to be a good man. But in these same terms, and by any measure we may care to invoke, he is hardly "worth it." And in these same terms, neither is the war itself.

Saving Private Ryan may indeed be the greatest war movie ever made. It provides undeniable evidence that Spielberg and his generation—call them the Baby Boomers, the generation of '68, the Vietnam generation, or whatever—understand what it was like for their fathers to fight in World War II. It even provides implicit evidence that they understand the stakes of World War II, and the rightness of World War II. But it leads one to suspect that, all the same, they would never have fought it themselves.

FOR FURTHER RESEARCH

Albert Auster and Leonard Quart, *How the War Was Remembered: Hollywood & Vietnam*. Westport, CT: Praeger, 1988.
  The first chapter provides historical background on war films in general; the rest of the book identifies major themes in Vietnam War movies.

Loren Baritz, *Backfire: A History of How American Culture Led Us into Vietnam and Made Us Fight the Way We Did*. Baltimore: Johns Hopkins University Press, 1998.
  Baritz argues that Americans' idealism and belief in the invincibility and moral supremacy of the United States were responsible for the Vietnam War.

Les Cleveland, *Dark Laughter: War in Song and Popular Culture*. Westport, CT: Praeger, 1994.
  Cleveland draws on military songs, folk songs, and popular music from World War I through Vietnam to explore the relationships between military life and society.

Gary Crowdus, ed., *A Political Companion to American Film*. Chicago: Lakeview Press, 1994.
  While this encyclopedia is not solely about war films, it does contain fairly detailed entries on anticommunism and the film industry, World War II films, and Vietnam films.

Leslie Midkiff Debauche, *Reel Patriotism: The Movies and World War I*. Madison: University of Wisconsin Press, 1997.
  Debauche examines the influence of the American film industry during World War I and in the decade following the conflict.

Bernard F. Dick, *The Star-Spangled Screen: The American World War II Film*. Lexington: University Press of Kentucky, 1996.
  Dick examines the historical accuracy (or lack thereof) of films about the Third Reich, the Resistance, the Holocaust, and the major military campaigns of World War II.

Linda Dittmar and Gene Michaud, eds., *From Hanoi to Hollywood: The Vietnam War and American Film*. New Brunswick, NJ: Rutgers University Press, 1990.

This anthology on Vietnam War films emphasizes how such films can influence people's remembrance of the war.

Thomas Doherty, *Projections of War: Hollywood, American Culture, and World War II.* New York: Columbia University Press, 1993.
Chapters in this book explore the evolution of World War II films and their depiction of the enemy, women, and blacks.

Tom Engelhardt, *The End of Victory Culture: Cold War America and the Disillusioning of a Generation.* New York: BasicBooks, 1995.
Citing movies, television, and even toy soldiers to support his view, Engelhardt argues that Americans have always viewed war as "cowboys and Indians," with the United States always viewing the enemy as a nonwhite, technically inferior people.

Joyce A. Evans, *Celluloid Mushroom Clouds: Hollywood and the Atomic Bomb.* Boulder, CO: Westview Press, 1998.
In somewhat abstract terms, Evans analyzes atomic imagery in films made between 1947 and 1961 to argue that Hollywood used the bomb to subtly criticize Cold War ideology.

Brock Garland, *War Movies.* New York: Facts On File, 1987.
After an overview on the history and art of war films, Garland provides an alphabetical listing of major war movies, with plot summaries and critical commentary accompanying each entry.

James William Gibson, *Warrior Dreams: Violence and Manhood in Post-Vietnam America.* New York: Hill and Wang, 1994.
Gibson details how, in the wake of Vietnam, a "war consumer culture" has emerged, with American men eager for war themes in television, movies, video games, and other forms of entertainment.

Kevin Hillstrom and Laurie Collier Hillstrom, *The Vietnam Experience: A Concise Encyclopedia of American Literature, Songs, and Film.* Westport, CT: Greenwood Press, 1998.
Each entry in this volume provides a description of a specific book, song, or film, along with background on its pertinence to the Vietnam War.

M. Paul Holsinger, ed., *War and American Popular Culture: An Encyclopedia.* Westport, CT: Greenwood Press, 1999.
An excellent overview of war themes in popular culture; Holsinger provides entries on paintings, authors, books, plays, songs, films,

and more for each of America's major and minor wars from the Revolution through the Persian Gulf War.

Peter G. Jones, *War and the Novelist: Appraising the American War Novel*. Columbia: University of Missouri Press, 1976.
The primary focus of this literary critique is on novels of World War II, the Korean War, and Vietnam; chapters examine the structure of war novels and how they deal with sex, violence, authority, and the role of technology.

Michael Lee Lanning, *Vietnam at the Movies*. New York: Fawcett Columbine, 1994.
Lanning begins with a history of combat films before moving on to a comprehensive critique of movies about Vietnam.

Alf Louvre and Jeffrey Walsh, eds., *Tell Me Lies About Vietnam: Cultural Battles for the Meaning of the War*. Philadelphia: Open University Press, 1988.
Essays in this anthology explore how the Vietnam War has been represented in films, novels, comic books, political cartoons, music, poetry, and drama.

Richard Maltby, ed., *Passing Parade: A History of Popular Culture in the Twentieth Century*. New York: Oxford University Press, 1989.
Filled with photographs, this coffee-table book provides a broad overview of twentieth-century popular culture, with appropriate sections on the major wars of the period.

Stewart O'Nan, *The Vietnam Reader: The Definitive Collection of American Fiction and Nonfiction on the War*. New York: Anchor Books, 1998.
This anthology contains fiction and nonfiction on the war from well-known writers, lyrics from Vietnam protest songs, and essays on the major films about Vietnam.

Toni A. Perrine, *Film and the Nuclear Age: Representing Cultural Anxiety*. New York: Garland, 1998.
Perrine examines various themes in films about nuclear war from the 1950s through the 1980s. The book includes a chronology and a list of nuclear films by year.

David Platt, *Celluloid Power: Social Film Criticism from* The Birth of a Nation *to* Judgment at Nuremberg. Metuchen, NJ: Scarecrow Press, 1992.

Essays in this anthology include "American Propaganda Films of the First World War," "World War II and the American Film," "The Screen and the Holocaust," and "Stanley Kubrick's *Dr. Strangelove.*"

Michael S. Sherry, *In the Shadow of War: The United States Since the 1930s.* New Haven, CT: Yale University Press, 1995.
Sherry details the expansion of the American armed forces since the 1930s, and how this has affected the economy, people's daily lives, and the nation's willingness to go to war.

Colin Shindler, *Hollywood Goes to War: Films and American Society, 1930–1952.* Boston: Routledge and Kegan Paul, 1979.
Shindler provides a detailed narrative account of the film industry's response to World War II.

Lawrence H. Suid, *Guts and Glory: Great American War Movies.* Reading, MA: Addison-Wesley, 1978.
Suid offers a film-by-film synopsis of major war movies and their social context from World War I to Vietnam.